C-4606   CAREER EXAMINATION SERIES

*This is your
PASSBOOK for...*

Postal Automotive Technician Exam (944)

*Test Preparation Study Guide
Questions & Answers*

NATIONAL LEARNING CORPORATION®

COPYRIGHT NOTICE

This book is SOLELY intended for, is sold ONLY to, and its use is RESTRICTED to individual, bona fide applicants or candidates who qualify by virtue of having seriously filed applications for appropriate license, certificate, professional and/or promotional advancement, higher school matriculation, scholarship, or other legitimate requirements of education and/or governmental authorities.

This book is NOT intended for use, class instruction, tutoring, training, duplication, copying, reprinting, excerption, or adaptation, etc., by:

1) Other publishers
2) Proprietors and/or Instructors of "Coaching" and/or Preparatory Courses
3) Personnel and/or Training Divisions of commercial, industrial, and governmental organizations
4) Schools, colleges, or universities and/or their departments and staffs, including teachers and other personnel
5) Testing Agencies or Bureaus
6) Study groups which seek by the purchase of a single volume to copy and/or duplicate and/or adapt this material for use by the group as a whole without having purchased individual volumes for each of the members of the group
7) Et al.

Such persons would be in violation of appropriate Federal and State statutes.

PROVISION OF LICENSING AGREEMENTS – Recognized educational, commercial, industrial, and governmental institutions and organizations, and others legitimately engaged in educational pursuits, including training, testing, and measurement activities, may address request for a licensing agreement to the copyright owners, who will determine whether, and under what conditions, including fees and charges, the materials in this book may be used them. In other words, a licensing facility exists for the legitimate use of the material in this book on other than an individual basis. However, it is asseverated and affirmed here that the material in this book CANNOT be used without the receipt of the express permission of such a licensing agreement from the Publishers. Inquiries re licensing should be addressed to the company, attention rights and permissions department.

All rights reserved, including the right of reproduction in whole or in part, in any form or by any means, electronic or mechanical, including photocopying, recording, or by any information storage and retrieval system, without permission in writing from the Publisher.

Copyright © 2024 by
National Learning Corporation

212 Michael Drive, Syosset, NY 11791
(516) 921-8888 • www.passbooks.com
E-mail: info@passbooks.com

PUBLISHED IN THE UNITED STATES OF AMERICA

PASSBOOK® SERIES

THE *PASSBOOK® SERIES* has been created to prepare applicants and candidates for the ultimate academic battlefield – the examination room.

At some time in our lives, each and every one of us may be required to take an examination – for validation, matriculation, admission, qualification, registration, certification, or licensure.

Based on the assumption that every applicant or candidate has met the basic formal educational standards, has taken the required number of courses, and read the necessary texts, the *PASSBOOK® SERIES* furnishes the one special preparation which may assure passing with confidence, instead of failing with insecurity. Examination questions – together with answers – are furnished as the basic vehicle for study so that the mysteries of the examination and its compounding difficulties may be eliminated or diminished by a sure method.

This book is meant to help you pass your examination provided that you qualify and are serious in your objective.

The entire field is reviewed through the huge store of content information which is succinctly presented through a provocative and challenging approach – the question-and-answer method.

A climate of success is established by furnishing the correct answers at the end of each test.

You soon learn to recognize types of questions, forms of questions, and patterns of questioning. You may even begin to anticipate expected outcomes.

You perceive that many questions are repeated or adapted so that you can gain acute insights, which may enable you to score many sure points.

You learn how to confront new questions, or types of questions, and to attack them confidently and work out the correct answers.

You note objectives and emphases, and recognize pitfalls and dangers, so that you may make positive educational adjustments.

Moreover, you are kept fully informed in relation to new concepts, methods, practices, and directions in the field.

You discover that you are actually taking the examination all the time: you are preparing for the examination by "taking" an examination, not by reading extraneous and/or supererogatory textbooks.

In short, this PASSBOOK®, used directedly, should be an important factor in helping you to pass your test.

POSTAL AUTOMOTIVE TECHNICIAN EXAM (944)

POSITION DESCRIPTION

Postal Automotive Technicians diagnose the operations of a wide variety of vehicles in the postal fleet. Typical duties include troubleshooting and diagnosing vehicle operations using a variety of tools and test equipment.

DUTIES AND RESPONSIBILITIES

1. Diagnoses operating difficulties on a variety of vehicles and performs operational checks on engines; its major supporting systems, parts, components, assemblies, including emissions systems, electrical, computer and electronic controlled components.
2. Performs various computerized and electronic diagnostic tests using specialized equipment; interprets trouble codes and other information from electronic scanners and test analyzers; uses reference materials such as service manuals and wiring schematics to determine operational difficulties, driveability problems and evaluates performance efficiency.
3. Conducts visual and auditory vehicle inspections, road calls and road tests before and after maintenance and repairs; annotates vehicle problems on work orders.
4. Provides technical guidance and instructions to mechanics and technicians on more difficult repairs and in the use of specialized computer-aided diagnostic equipment.
5. Performs maintenance and repairs resulting from normal preventive maintenance inspections.
6. Prepares and updates vehicle records, maintains vehicle records; annotates labor time, parts, and/or equipment and other pertinent data on work orders.
7. Performs engine tune-ups; removes, replaces, adjusts, cleans parts, components, assemblies and accessories; uses a variety of specialized test equipment to adjust systems and components to prescribed operating tolerances.
8. Troubleshoots malfunctioning vehicles resulting from road calls and identifies improperly functioning part(s) and repairs or replaces.
9. Repairs and replaces major components including transmissions, differentials, brake systems, power assist units, steering and suspension assemblies.
10. Performs other job related duties and responsibilities in support of primary duties.
11. Follows all established safety practices and procedures; complies with all postal, local, state and federal environmental regulations and policies

SAMPLE QUESTIONS

1. In addition to vacuum, which of the following represents one means of opening an Exhaust Gas Recirculation (EGR) system valve?
    A. Electricity
    B. Hydraulic pressure
    C. Manual linkage
    D. Compression spring

2. A technician is performing a four-gas analyzer test on a vehicle and finds a high hydrocarbon (HC) reading, with the engine misfiring only at idle. What is most likely the cause?
    A. Leaking intake manifold
    B. Exhaust Gas Recirculation (EGR) valve that does not fully close
    C. Secondary ignition wire shorting
    D. Partially clogged fuel injector

3. When a transmission in the park position emits a high-pitched whine that increases With engine revolutions per minute (RPM), what is the most likely cause?
    A. A bad front pump
    B. A loose torque converter
    C. Misadjusted park pawl
    D. A worn sprag unit

4. It is NOT necessary to remove an automatic transmission to make which of the following repairs?
    A. Front pump seal
    B. Governor assembly
    C. Rear clutch pack
    D. Stator support assembly

5. A wet compression test is used to isolate which engine defect?
    A. Leaking head gasket
    B. Worn valve seats
    C. Worn valve seals
    D. Worn piston rings

6. Which three of the following are most likely to be caused by excessive fuel-pump pressure?
    1. The carburetor float needle held off its seat
    2. High gasoline level in the carburetor float chamber
    3. Air lock in the fuel line
    4. Increased gas consumption
    A. 1, 2, and 3, but not 4
    B. 1, 2, and 4, but not 3
    C. 1, 3, and 4, but not 2
    D. 2, 3, and 4, but not 1

CORRECT ANSWERS:

1. A   4. B
2. B   5. D
3. A   6. B

HOW TO TAKE A TEST

I. YOU MUST PASS AN EXAMINATION

A. WHAT EVERY CANDIDATE SHOULD KNOW

Examination applicants often ask us for help in preparing for the written test. What can I study in advance? What kinds of questions will be asked? How will the test be given? How will the papers be graded?

As an applicant for a civil service examination, you may be wondering about some of these things. Our purpose here is to suggest effective methods of advance study and to describe civil service examinations.

Your chances for success on this examination can be increased if you know how to prepare. Those "pre-examination jitters" can be reduced if you know what to expect. You can even experience an adventure in good citizenship if you know why civil service exams are given.

B. WHY ARE CIVIL SERVICE EXAMINATIONS GIVEN?

Civil service examinations are important to you in two ways. As a citizen, you want public jobs filled by employees who know how to do their work. As a job seeker, you want a fair chance to compete for that job on an equal footing with other candidates. The best-known means of accomplishing this two-fold goal is the competitive examination.

Exams are widely publicized throughout the nation. They may be administered for jobs in federal, state, city, municipal, town or village governments or agencies.

Any citizen may apply, with some limitations, such as the age or residence of applicants. Your experience and education may be reviewed to see whether you meet the requirements for the particular examination. When these requirements exist, they are reasonable and applied consistently to all applicants. Thus, a competitive examination may cause you some uneasiness now, but it is your privilege and safeguard.

C. HOW ARE CIVIL SERVICE EXAMS DEVELOPED?

Examinations are carefully written by trained technicians who are specialists in the field known as "psychological measurement," in consultation with recognized authorities in the field of work that the test will cover. These experts recommend the subject matter areas or skills to be tested; only those knowledges or skills important to your success on the job are included. The most reliable books and source materials available are used as references. Together, the experts and technicians judge the difficulty level of the questions.

Test technicians know how to phrase questions so that the problem is clearly stated. Their ethics do not permit "trick" or "catch" questions. Questions may have been tried out on sample groups, or subjected to statistical analysis, to determine their usefulness.

Written tests are often used in combination with performance tests, ratings of training and experience, and oral interviews. All of these measures combine to form the best-known means of finding the right person for the right job.

II. HOW TO PASS THE WRITTEN TEST

A. NATURE OF THE EXAMINATION

To prepare intelligently for civil service examinations, you should know how they differ from school examinations you have taken. In school you were assigned certain definite pages to read or subjects to cover. The examination questions were quite detailed and usually emphasized memory. Civil service exams, on the other hand, try to discover your present ability to perform the duties of a position, plus your potentiality to learn these duties. In other words, a civil service exam attempts to predict how successful you will be. Questions cover such a broad area that they cannot be as minute and detailed as school exam questions.

In the public service similar kinds of work, or positions, are grouped together in one "class." This process is known as *position-classification*. All the positions in a class are paid according to the salary range for that class. One class title covers all of these positions, and they are all tested by the same examination.

B. FOUR BASIC STEPS

1) Study the announcement

How, then, can you know what subjects to study? Our best answer is: "Learn as much as possible about the class of positions for which you've applied." The exam will test the knowledge, skills and abilities needed to do the work.

Your most valuable source of information about the position you want is the official exam announcement. This announcement lists the training and experience qualifications. Check these standards and apply only if you come reasonably close to meeting them.

The brief description of the position in the examination announcement offers some clues to the subjects which will be tested. Think about the job itself. Review the duties in your mind. Can you perform them, or are there some in which you are rusty? Fill in the blank spots in your preparation.

Many jurisdictions preview the written test in the exam announcement by including a section called "Knowledge and Abilities Required," "Scope of the Examination," or some similar heading. Here you will find out specifically what fields will be tested.

2) Review your own background

Once you learn in general what the position is all about, and what you need to know to do the work, ask yourself which subjects you already know fairly well and which need improvement. You may wonder whether to concentrate on improving your strong areas or on building some background in your fields of weakness. When the announcement has specified "some knowledge" or "considerable knowledge," or has used adjectives like "beginning principles of…" or "advanced … methods," you can get a clue as to the number and difficulty of questions to be asked in any given field. More questions, and hence broader coverage, would be included for those subjects which are more important in the work. Now weigh your strengths and weaknesses against the job requirements and prepare accordingly.

3) Determine the level of the position

Another way to tell how intensively you should prepare is to understand the level of the job for which you are applying. Is it the entering level? In other words, is this the position in which beginners in a field of work are hired? Or is it an intermediate or advanced level? Sometimes this is indicated by such words as "Junior" or "Senior" in the class title. Other jurisdictions use Roman numerals to designate the level – Clerk I, Clerk II, for example. The word "Supervisor" sometimes appears in the title. If the level is not indicated by the title, check the description of duties. Will you be working under very close supervision, or will you have responsibility for independent decisions in this work?

4) Choose appropriate study materials

Now that you know the subjects to be examined and the relative amount of each subject to be covered, you can choose suitable study materials. For beginning level jobs, or even advanced ones, if you have a pronounced weakness in some aspect of your training, read a modern, standard textbook in that field. Be sure it is up to date and has general coverage. Such books are normally available at your library, and the librarian will be glad to help you locate one. For entry-level positions, questions of appropriate difficulty are chosen – neither highly advanced questions, nor those too simple. Such questions require careful thought but not advanced training.

If the position for which you are applying is technical or advanced, you will read more advanced, specialized material. If you are already familiar with the basic principles of your field, elementary textbooks would waste your time. Concentrate on advanced textbooks and technical periodicals. Think through the concepts and review difficult problems in your field.

These are all general sources. You can get more ideas on your own initiative, following these leads. For example, training manuals and publications of the government agency which employs workers in your field can be useful, particularly for technical and professional positions. A letter or visit to the government department involved may result in more specific study suggestions, and certainly will provide you with a more definite idea of the exact nature of the position you are seeking.

III. KINDS OF TESTS

Tests are used for purposes other than measuring knowledge and ability to perform specified duties. For some positions, it is equally important to test ability to make adjustments to new situations or to profit from training. In others, basic mental abilities not dependent on information are essential. Questions which test these things may not appear as pertinent to the duties of the position as those which test for knowledge and information. Yet they are often highly important parts of a fair examination. For very general questions, it is almost impossible to help you direct your study efforts. What we can do is to point out some of the more common of these general abilities needed in public service positions and describe some typical questions.

1) General information

Broad, general information has been found useful for predicting job success in some kinds of work. This is tested in a variety of ways, from vocabulary lists to questions about current events. Basic background in some field of work, such as sociology or economics, may be sampled in a group of questions. Often these are principles which have become familiar to most persons through exposure rather than through formal training. It is difficult to advise you how to study for these questions; being alert to the world around you is our best suggestion.

2) Verbal ability

An example of an ability needed in many positions is verbal or language ability. Verbal ability is, in brief, the ability to use and understand words. Vocabulary and grammar tests are typical measures of this ability. Reading comprehension or paragraph interpretation questions are common in many kinds of civil service tests. You are given a paragraph of written material and asked to find its central meaning.

3) Numerical ability

Number skills can be tested by the familiar arithmetic problem, by checking paired lists of numbers to see which are alike and which are different, or by interpreting charts and graphs. In the latter test, a graph may be printed in the test booklet which you are asked to use as the basis for answering questions.

4) Observation

A popular test for law-enforcement positions is the observation test. A picture is shown to you for several minutes, then taken away. Questions about the picture test your ability to observe both details and larger elements.

5) Following directions

In many positions in the public service, the employee must be able to carry out written instructions dependably and accurately. You may be given a chart with several columns, each column listing a variety of information. The questions require you to carry out directions involving the information given in the chart.

6) Skills and aptitudes

Performance tests effectively measure some manual skills and aptitudes. When the skill is one in which you are trained, such as typing or shorthand, you can practice. These tests are often very much like those given in business school or high school courses. For many of the other skills and aptitudes, however, no short-time preparation can be made. Skills and abilities natural to you or that you have developed throughout your lifetime are being tested.

Many of the general questions just described provide all the data needed to answer the questions and ask you to use your reasoning ability to find the answers. Your best preparation for these tests, as well as for tests of facts and ideas, is to be at your physical and mental best. You, no doubt, have your own methods of getting into an exam-taking mood and keeping "in shape." The next section lists some ideas on this subject.

IV. KINDS OF QUESTIONS

Only rarely is the "essay" question, which you answer in narrative form, used in civil service tests. Civil service tests are usually of the short-answer type. Full instructions for answering these questions will be given to you at the examination. But in case this is your first experience with short-answer questions and separate answer sheets, here is what you need to know:

1) Multiple-choice Questions

Most popular of the short-answer questions is the "multiple choice" or "best answer" question. It can be used, for example, to test for factual knowledge, ability to solve problems or judgment in meeting situations found at work.

A multiple-choice question is normally one of three types—
- It can begin with an incomplete statement followed by several possible endings. You are to find the one ending which *best* completes the statement, although some of the others may not be entirely wrong.
- It can also be a complete statement in the form of a question which is answered by choosing one of the statements listed.

- It can be in the form of a problem – again you select the best answer.

Here is an example of a multiple-choice question with a discussion which should give you some clues as to the method for choosing the right answer:

When an employee has a complaint about his assignment, the action which will *best* help him overcome his difficulty is to
- A. discuss his difficulty with his coworkers
- B. take the problem to the head of the organization
- C. take the problem to the person who gave him the assignment
- D. say nothing to anyone about his complaint

In answering this question, you should study each of the choices to find which is best. Consider choice "A" – Certainly an employee may discuss his complaint with fellow employees, but no change or improvement can result, and the complaint remains unresolved. Choice "B" is a poor choice since the head of the organization probably does not know what assignment you have been given, and taking your problem to him is known as "going over the head" of the supervisor. The supervisor, or person who made the assignment, is the person who can clarify it or correct any injustice. Choice "C" is, therefore, correct. To say nothing, as in choice "D," is unwise. Supervisors have and interest in knowing the problems employees are facing, and the employee is seeking a solution to his problem.

2) True/False Questions

The "true/false" or "right/wrong" form of question is sometimes used. Here a complete statement is given. Your job is to decide whether the statement is right or wrong.

SAMPLE: A roaming cell-phone call to a nearby city costs less than a non-roaming call to a distant city.

This statement is wrong, or false, since roaming calls are more expensive.

This is not a complete list of all possible question forms, although most of the others are variations of these common types. You will always get complete directions for answering questions. Be sure you understand *how* to mark your answers – ask questions until you do.

V. RECORDING YOUR ANSWERS

Computer terminals are used more and more today for many different kinds of exams.

For an examination with very few applicants, you may be told to record your answers in the test booklet itself. Separate answer sheets are much more common. If this separate answer sheet is to be scored by machine – and this is often the case – it is highly important that you mark your answers correctly in order to get credit.

An electronic scoring machine is often used in civil service offices because of the speed with which papers can be scored. Machine-scored answer sheets must be marked with a pencil, which will be given to you. This pencil has a high graphite content which responds to the electronic scoring machine. As a matter of fact, stray dots may register as answers, so do not let your pencil rest on the answer sheet while you are pondering the correct answer. Also, if your pencil lead breaks or is otherwise defective, ask for another.

Since the answer sheet will be dropped in a slot in the scoring machine, be careful not to bend the corners or get the paper crumpled.

The answer sheet normally has five vertical columns of numbers, with 30 numbers to a column. These numbers correspond to the question numbers in your test booklet. After each number, going across the page are four or five pairs of dotted lines. These short dotted lines have small letters or numbers above them. The first two pairs may also have a "T" or "F" above the letters. This indicates that the first two pairs only are to be used if the questions are of the true-false type. If the questions are multiple choice, disregard the "T" and "F" and pay attention only to the small letters or numbers.

Answer your questions in the manner of the sample that follows:

    32. The largest city in the United States is
         A. Washington, D.C.
         B. New York City
         C. Chicago
         D. Detroit
         E. San Francisco

1) Choose the answer you think is best. (New York City is the largest, so "B" is correct.)
2) Find the row of dotted lines numbered the same as the question you are answering. (Find row number 32)
3) Find the pair of dotted lines corresponding to the answer. (Find the pair of lines under the mark "B.")
4) Make a solid black mark between the dotted lines.

VI. BEFORE THE TEST

Common sense will help you find procedures to follow to get ready for an examination. Too many of us, however, overlook these sensible measures. Indeed, nervousness and fatigue have been found to be the most serious reasons why applicants fail to do their best on civil service tests. Here is a list of reminders:

- Begin your preparation early – Don't wait until the last minute to go scurrying around for books and materials or to find out what the position is all about.
- Prepare continuously – An hour a night for a week is better than an all-night cram session. This has been definitely established. What is more, a night a week for a month will return better dividends than crowding your study into a shorter period of time.
- Locate the place of the exam – You have been sent a notice telling you when and where to report for the examination. If the location is in a different town or otherwise unfamiliar to you, it would be well to inquire the best route and learn something about the building.
- Relax the night before the test – Allow your mind to rest. Do not study at all that night. Plan some mild recreation or diversion; then go to bed early and get a good night's sleep.
- Get up early enough to make a leisurely trip to the place for the test – This way unforeseen events, traffic snarls, unfamiliar buildings, etc. will not upset you.
- Dress comfortably – A written test is not a fashion show. You will be known by number and not by name, so wear something comfortable.

- Leave excess paraphernalia at home – Shopping bags and odd bundles will get in your way. You need bring only the items mentioned in the official notice you received; usually everything you need is provided. Do not bring reference books to the exam. They will only confuse those last minutes and be taken away from you when in the test room.
- Arrive somewhat ahead of time – If because of transportation schedules you must get there very early, bring a newspaper or magazine to take your mind off yourself while waiting.
- Locate the examination room – When you have found the proper room, you will be directed to the seat or part of the room where you will sit. Sometimes you are given a sheet of instructions to read while you are waiting. Do not fill out any forms until you are told to do so; just read them and be prepared.
- Relax and prepare to listen to the instructions
- If you have any physical problem that may keep you from doing your best, be sure to tell the test administrator. If you are sick or in poor health, you really cannot do your best on the exam. You can come back and take the test some other time.

VII. AT THE TEST

The day of the test is here and you have the test booklet in your hand. The temptation to get going is very strong. Caution! There is more to success than knowing the right answers. You must know how to identify your papers and understand variations in the type of short-answer question used in this particular examination. Follow these suggestions for maximum results from your efforts:

1) Cooperate with the monitor

The test administrator has a duty to create a situation in which you can be as much at ease as possible. He will give instructions, tell you when to begin, check to see that you are marking your answer sheet correctly, and so on. He is not there to guard you, although he will see that your competitors do not take unfair advantage. He wants to help you do your best.

2) Listen to all instructions

Don't jump the gun! Wait until you understand all directions. In most civil service tests you get more time than you need to answer the questions. So don't be in a hurry. Read each word of instructions until you clearly understand the meaning. Study the examples, listen to all announcements and follow directions. Ask questions if you do not understand what to do.

3) Identify your papers

Civil service exams are usually identified by number only. You will be assigned a number; you must not put your name on your test papers. Be sure to copy your number correctly. Since more than one exam may be given, copy your exact examination title.

4) Plan your time

Unless you are told that a test is a "speed" or "rate of work" test, speed itself is usually not important. Time enough to answer all the questions will be provided, but this does not mean that you have all day. An overall time limit has been set. Divide the total time (in minutes) by the number of questions to determine the approximate time you have for each question.

5) Do not linger over difficult questions

If you come across a difficult question, mark it with a paper clip (useful to have along) and come back to it when you have been through the booklet. One caution if you do this – be sure to skip a number on your answer sheet as well. Check often to be sure that you have not lost your place and that you are marking in the row numbered the same as the question you are answering.

6) Read the questions

Be sure you know what the question asks! Many capable people are unsuccessful because they failed to *read* the questions correctly.

7) Answer all questions

Unless you have been instructed that a penalty will be deducted for incorrect answers, it is better to guess than to omit a question.

8) Speed tests

It is often better NOT to guess on speed tests. It has been found that on timed tests people are tempted to spend the last few seconds before time is called in marking answers at random – without even reading them – in the hope of picking up a few extra points. To discourage this practice, the instructions may warn you that your score will be "corrected" for guessing. That is, a penalty will be applied. The incorrect answers will be deducted from the correct ones, or some other penalty formula will be used.

9) Review your answers

If you finish before time is called, go back to the questions you guessed or omitted to give them further thought. Review other answers if you have time.

10) Return your test materials

If you are ready to leave before others have finished or time is called, take ALL your materials to the monitor and leave quietly. Never take any test material with you. The monitor can discover whose papers are not complete, and taking a test booklet may be grounds for disqualification.

VIII. EXAMINATION TECHNIQUES

1) Read the general instructions carefully. These are usually printed on the first page of the exam booklet. As a rule, these instructions refer to the timing of the examination; the fact that you should not start work until the signal and must stop work at a signal, etc. If there are any *special* instructions, such as a choice of questions to be answered, make sure that you note this instruction carefully.

2) When you are ready to start work on the examination, that is as soon as the signal has been given, read the instructions to each question booklet, underline any key words or phrases, such as *least, best, outline, describe* and the like. In this way you will tend to answer as requested rather than discover on reviewing your paper that you *listed without describing*, that you selected the *worst* choice rather than the *best* choice, etc.

3) If the examination is of the objective or multiple-choice type – that is, each question will also give a series of possible answers: A, B, C or D, and you are called upon to select the best answer and write the letter next to that answer on your answer paper – it is advisable to start answering each question in turn. There may be anywhere from 50 to 100 such questions in the three or four hours allotted and you can see how much time would be taken if you read through all the questions before beginning to answer any. Furthermore, if you come across a question or group of questions which you know would be difficult to answer, it would undoubtedly affect your handling of all the other questions.

4) If the examination is of the essay type and contains but a few questions, it is a moot point as to whether you should read all the questions before starting to answer any one. Of course, if you are given a choice – say five out of seven and the like – then it is essential to read all the questions so you can eliminate the two that are most difficult. If, however, you are asked to answer all the questions, there may be danger in trying to answer the easiest one first because you may find that you will spend too much time on it. The best technique is to answer the first question, then proceed to the second, etc.

5) Time your answers. Before the exam begins, write down the time it started, then add the time allowed for the examination and write down the time it must be completed, then divide the time available somewhat as follows:
   - If 3-1/2 hours are allowed, that would be 210 minutes. If you have 80 objective-type questions, that would be an average of 2-1/2 minutes per question. Allow yourself no more than 2 minutes per question, or a total of 160 minutes, which will permit about 50 minutes to review.
   - If for the time allotment of 210 minutes there are 7 essay questions to answer, that would average about 30 minutes a question. Give yourself only 25 minutes per question so that you have about 35 minutes to review.

6) The most important instruction is to *read each question* and make sure you know what is wanted. The second most important instruction is to *time yourself properly* so that you answer every question. The third most important instruction is to *answer every question*. Guess if you have to but include something for each question. Remember that you will receive no credit for a blank and will probably receive some credit if you write something in answer to an essay question. If you guess a letter – say "B" for a multiple-choice question – you may have guessed right. If you leave a blank as an answer to a multiple-choice question, the examiners may respect your feelings but it will not add a point to your score. Some exams may penalize you for wrong answers, so in such cases *only*, you may not want to guess unless you have some basis for your answer.

7) Suggestions
   a. Objective-type questions
      1. Examine the question booklet for proper sequence of pages and questions
      2. Read all instructions carefully
      3. Skip any question which seems too difficult; return to it after all other questions have been answered
      4. Apportion your time properly; do not spend too much time on any single question or group of questions

5. Note and underline key words – *all, most, fewest, least, best, worst, same, opposite,* etc.
6. Pay particular attention to negatives
7. Note unusual option, e.g., unduly long, short, complex, different or similar in content to the body of the question
8. Observe the use of "hedging" words – *probably, may, most likely,* etc.
9. Make sure that your answer is put next to the same number as the question
10. Do not second-guess unless you have good reason to believe the second answer is definitely more correct
11. Cross out original answer if you decide another answer is more accurate; do not erase until you are ready to hand your paper in
12. Answer all questions; guess unless instructed otherwise
13. Leave time for review

  b. Essay questions
1. Read each question carefully
2. Determine exactly what is wanted. Underline key words or phrases.
3. Decide on outline or paragraph answer
4. Include many different points and elements unless asked to develop any one or two points or elements
5. Show impartiality by giving pros and cons unless directed to select one side only
6. Make and write down any assumptions you find necessary to answer the questions
7. Watch your English, grammar, punctuation and choice of words
8. Time your answers; don't crowd material

8) Answering the essay question

Most essay questions can be answered by framing the specific response around several key words or ideas. Here are a few such key words or ideas:

M's: manpower, materials, methods, money, management
P's: purpose, program, policy, plan, procedure, practice, problems, pitfalls, personnel, public relations

  a. Six basic steps in handling problems:
1. Preliminary plan and background development
2. Collect information, data and facts
3. Analyze and interpret information, data and facts
4. Analyze and develop solutions as well as make recommendations
5. Prepare report and sell recommendations
6. Install recommendations and follow up effectiveness

  b. Pitfalls to avoid
1. *Taking things for granted* – A statement of the situation does not necessarily imply that each of the elements is necessarily true; for example, a complaint may be invalid and biased so that all that can be taken for granted is that a complaint has been registered

2. *Considering only one side of a situation* – Wherever possible, indicate several alternatives and then point out the reasons you selected the best one
3. *Failing to indicate follow up* – Whenever your answer indicates action on your part, make certain that you will take proper follow-up action to see how successful your recommendations, procedures or actions turn out to be
4. *Taking too long in answering any single question* – Remember to time your answers properly

IX. AFTER THE TEST

Scoring procedures differ in detail among civil service jurisdictions although the general principles are the same. Whether the papers are hand-scored or graded by machine we have described, they are nearly always graded by number. That is, the person who marks the paper knows only the number – never the name – of the applicant. Not until all the papers have been graded will they be matched with names. If other tests, such as training and experience or oral interview ratings have been given, scores will be combined. Different parts of the examination usually have different weights. For example, the written test might count 60 percent of the final grade, and a rating of training and experience 40 percent. In many jurisdictions, veterans will have a certain number of points added to their grades.

After the final grade has been determined, the names are placed in grade order and an eligible list is established. There are various methods for resolving ties between those who get the same final grade – probably the most common is to place first the name of the person whose application was received first. Job offers are made from the eligible list in the order the names appear on it. You will be notified of your grade and your rank as soon as all these computations have been made. This will be done as rapidly as possible.

People who are found to meet the requirements in the announcement are called "eligibles." Their names are put on a list of eligible candidates. An eligible's chances of getting a job depend on how high he stands on this list and how fast agencies are filling jobs from the list.

When a job is to be filled from a list of eligibles, the agency asks for the names of people on the list of eligibles for that job. When the civil service commission receives this request, it sends to the agency the names of the three people highest on this list. Or, if the job to be filled has specialized requirements, the office sends the agency the names of the top three persons who meet these requirements from the general list.

The appointing officer makes a choice from among the three people whose names were sent to him. If the selected person accepts the appointment, the names of the others are put back on the list to be considered for future openings.

That is the rule in hiring from all kinds of eligible lists, whether they are for typist, carpenter, chemist, or something else. For every vacancy, the appointing officer has his choice of any one of the top three eligibles on the list. This explains why the person whose name is on top of the list sometimes does not get an appointment when some of the persons lower on the list do. If the appointing officer chooses the second or third eligible, the No. 1 eligible does not get a job at once, but stays on the list until he is appointed or the list is terminated.

X. HOW TO PASS THE INTERVIEW TEST

The examination for which you applied requires an oral interview test. You have already taken the written test and you are now being called for the interview test – the final part of the formal examination.

You may think that it is not possible to prepare for an interview test and that there are no procedures to follow during an interview. Our purpose is to point out some things you can do in advance that will help you and some good rules to follow and pitfalls to avoid while you are being interviewed.

What is an interview supposed to test?

The written examination is designed to test the technical knowledge and competence of the candidate; the oral is designed to evaluate intangible qualities, not readily measured otherwise, and to establish a list showing the relative fitness of each candidate – as measured against his competitors – for the position sought. Scoring is not on the basis of "right" and "wrong," but on a sliding scale of values ranging from "not passable" to "outstanding." As a matter of fact, it is possible to achieve a relatively low score without a single "incorrect" answer because of evident weakness in the qualities being measured.

Occasionally, an examination may consist entirely of an oral test – either an individual or a group oral. In such cases, information is sought concerning the technical knowledges and abilities of the candidate, since there has been no written examination for this purpose. More commonly, however, an oral test is used to supplement a written examination.

Who conducts interviews?

The composition of oral boards varies among different jurisdictions. In nearly all, a representative of the personnel department serves as chairman. One of the members of the board may be a representative of the department in which the candidate would work. In some cases, "outside experts" are used, and, frequently, a businessman or some other representative of the general public is asked to serve. Labor and management or other special groups may be represented. The aim is to secure the services of experts in the appropriate field.

However the board is composed, it is a good idea (and not at all improper or unethical) to ascertain in advance of the interview who the members are and what groups they represent. When you are introduced to them, you will have some idea of their backgrounds and interests, and at least you will not stutter and stammer over their names.

What should be done before the interview?

While knowledge about the board members is useful and takes some of the surprise element out of the interview, there is other preparation which is more substantive. It *is* possible to prepare for an oral interview – in several ways:

1) Keep a copy of your application and review it carefully before the interview

This may be the only document before the oral board, and the starting point of the interview. Know what education and experience you have listed there, and the sequence and dates of all of it. Sometimes the board will ask you to review the highlights of your experience for them; you should not have to hem and haw doing it.

2) Study the class specification and the examination announcement

Usually, the oral board has one or both of these to guide them. The qualities, characteristics or knowledges required by the position sought are stated in these documents. They offer valuable clues as to the nature of the oral interview. For example, if the job involves supervisory responsibilities, the announcement will usually indicate that knowledge of modern supervisory methods and the qualifications of the candidate as a supervisor will be tested. If so, you can expect such questions, frequently in the form of a hypothetical situation which you are expected to solve. NEVER go into an oral without knowledge of the duties and responsibilities of the job you seek.

3) Think through each qualification required
Try to visualize the kind of questions you would ask if you were a board member. How well could you answer them? Try especially to appraise your own knowledge and background in each area, *measured against the job sought*, and identify any areas in which you are weak. Be critical and realistic – do not flatter yourself.

4) Do some general reading in areas in which you feel you may be weak
For example, if the job involves supervision and your past experience has NOT, some general reading in supervisory methods and practices, particularly in the field of human relations, might be useful. Do NOT study agency procedures or detailed manuals. The oral board will be testing your understanding and capacity, not your memory.

5) Get a good night's sleep and watch your general health and mental attitude
You will want a clear head at the interview. Take care of a cold or any other minor ailment, and of course, no hangovers.

What should be done on the day of the interview?
Now comes the day of the interview itself. Give yourself plenty of time to get there. Plan to arrive somewhat ahead of the scheduled time, particularly if your appointment is in the fore part of the day. If a previous candidate fails to appear, the board might be ready for you a bit early. By early afternoon an oral board is almost invariably behind schedule if there are many candidates, and you may have to wait. Take along a book or magazine to read, or your application to review, but leave any extraneous material in the waiting room when you go in for your interview. In any event, relax and compose yourself.

The matter of dress is important. The board is forming impressions about you – from your experience, your manners, your attitude, and your appearance. Give your personal appearance careful attention. Dress your best, but not your flashiest. Choose conservative, appropriate clothing, and be sure it is immaculate. This is a business interview, and your appearance should indicate that you regard it as such. Besides, being well groomed and properly dressed will help boost your confidence.

Sooner or later, someone will call your name and escort you into the interview room. *This is it.* From here on you are on your own. It is too late for any more preparation. But remember, you asked for this opportunity to prove your fitness, and you are here because your request was granted.

What happens when you go in?
The usual sequence of events will be as follows: The clerk (who is often the board stenographer) will introduce you to the chairman of the oral board, who will introduce you to the other members of the board. Acknowledge the introductions before you sit down. Do not be surprised if you find a microphone facing you or a stenotypist sitting by. Oral interviews are usually recorded in the event of an appeal or other review.

Usually the chairman of the board will open the interview by reviewing the highlights of your education and work experience from your application – primarily for the benefit of the other members of the board, as well as to get the material into the record. Do not interrupt or comment unless there is an error or significant misinterpretation; if that is the case, do not hesitate. But do not quibble about insignificant matters. Also, he will usually ask you some question about your education, experience or your present job – partly to get you to start talking and to establish the interviewing "rapport." He may start the actual questioning, or turn it over to one of the other members. Frequently, each member undertakes the questioning on a particular area, one in which he is perhaps most competent, so you can expect each member to participate in the examination. Because time is limited, you may also expect some rather abrupt switches in the direction the questioning takes, so do not be upset by it. Normally, a board member will not pursue a single line of questioning unless he discovers a particular strength or weakness.

After each member has participated, the chairman will usually ask whether any member has any further questions, then will ask you if you have anything you wish to add. Unless you are expecting this question, it may floor you. Worse, it may start you off on an extended, extemporaneous speech. The board is not usually seeking more information. The question is principally to offer you a last opportunity to present further qualifications or to indicate that you have nothing to add. So, if you feel that a significant qualification or characteristic has been overlooked, it is proper to point it out in a sentence or so. Do not compliment the board on the thoroughness of their examination – they have been sketchy, and you know it. If you wish, merely say, "No thank you, I have nothing further to add." This is a point where you can "talk yourself out" of a good impression or fail to present an important bit of information. Remember, *you close the interview yourself*.

The chairman will then say, "That is all, Mr. _____, thank you." Do not be startled; the interview is over, and quicker than you think. Thank him, gather your belongings and take your leave. Save your sigh of relief for the other side of the door.

How to put your best foot forward

Throughout this entire process, you may feel that the board individually and collectively is trying to pierce your defenses, seek out your hidden weaknesses and embarrass and confuse you. Actually, this is not true. They are obliged to make an appraisal of your qualifications for the job you are seeking, and they want to see you in your best light. Remember, they must interview all candidates and a non-cooperative candidate may become a failure in spite of their best efforts to bring out his qualifications. Here are 15 suggestions that will help you:

1) Be natural – Keep your attitude confident, not cocky

If you are not confident that you can do the job, do not expect the board to be. Do not apologize for your weaknesses, try to bring out your strong points. The board is interested in a positive, not negative, presentation. Cockiness will antagonize any board member and make him wonder if you are covering up a weakness by a false show of strength.

2) Get comfortable, but don't lounge or sprawl

Sit erectly but not stiffly. A careless posture may lead the board to conclude that you are careless in other things, or at least that you are not impressed by the importance of the occasion. Either conclusion is natural, even if incorrect. Do not fuss with your clothing, a pencil or an ashtray. Your hands may occasionally be useful to emphasize a point; do not let them become a point of distraction.

3) Do not wisecrack or make small talk

This is a serious situation, and your attitude should show that you consider it as such. Further, the time of the board is limited – they do not want to waste it, and neither should you.

4) Do not exaggerate your experience or abilities

In the first place, from information in the application or other interviews and sources, the board may know more about you than you think. Secondly, you probably will not get away with it. An experienced board is rather adept at spotting such a situation, so do not take the chance.

5) If you know a board member, do not make a point of it, yet do not hide it

Certainly you are not fooling him, and probably not the other members of the board. Do not try to take advantage of your acquaintanceship – it will probably do you little good.

6) Do not dominate the interview

Let the board do that. They will give you the clues – do not assume that you have to do all the talking. Realize that the board has a number of questions to ask you, and do not try to take up all the interview time by showing off your extensive knowledge of the answer to the first one.

7) Be attentive

You only have 20 minutes or so, and you should keep your attention at its sharpest throughout. When a member is addressing a problem or question to you, give him your undivided attention. Address your reply principally to him, but do not exclude the other board members.

8) Do not interrupt

A board member may be stating a problem for you to analyze. He will ask you a question when the time comes. Let him state the problem, and wait for the question.

9) Make sure you understand the question

Do not try to answer until you are sure what the question is. If it is not clear, restate it in your own words or ask the board member to clarify it for you. However, do not haggle about minor elements.

10) Reply promptly but not hastily

A common entry on oral board rating sheets is "candidate responded readily," or "candidate hesitated in replies." Respond as promptly and quickly as you can, but do not jump to a hasty, ill-considered answer.

11) Do not be peremptory in your answers

A brief answer is proper – but do not fire your answer back. That is a losing game from your point of view. The board member can probably ask questions much faster than you can answer them.

12) Do not try to create the answer you think the board member wants

He is interested in what kind of mind you have and how it works – not in playing games. Furthermore, he can usually spot this practice and will actually grade you down on it.

13) Do not switch sides in your reply merely to agree with a board member

Frequently, a member will take a contrary position merely to draw you out and to see if you are willing and able to defend your point of view. Do not start a debate, yet do not surrender a good position. If a position is worth taking, it is worth defending.

14) Do not be afraid to admit an error in judgment if you are shown to be wrong

The board knows that you are forced to reply without any opportunity for careful consideration. Your answer may be demonstrably wrong. If so, admit it and get on with the interview.

15) Do not dwell at length on your present job

The opening question may relate to your present assignment. Answer the question but do not go into an extended discussion. You are being examined for a *new* job, not your present one. As a matter of fact, try to phrase ALL your answers in terms of the job for which you are being examined.

Basis of Rating

Probably you will forget most of these "do's" and "don'ts" when you walk into the oral interview room. Even remembering them all will not ensure you a passing grade. Perhaps you did not have the qualifications in the first place. But remembering them will help you to put your best foot forward, without treading on the toes of the board members.

Rumor and popular opinion to the contrary notwithstanding, an oral board wants you to make the best appearance possible. They know you are under pressure – but they also want to see how you respond to it as a guide to what your reaction would be under the pressures of the job you seek. They will be influenced by the degree of poise you display, the personal traits you show and the manner in which you respond.

ABOUT THIS BOOK

This book contains tests divided into Examination Sections. Go through each test, answering every question in the margin. We have also attached a sample answer sheet at the back of the book that can be removed and used. At the end of each test look at the answer key and check your answers. On the ones you got wrong, look at the right answer choice and learn. Do not fill in the answers first. Do not memorize the questions and answers, but understand the answer and principles involved. On your test, the questions will likely be different from the samples. Questions are changed and new ones added. If you understand these past questions you should have success with any changes that arise. Tests may consist of several types of questions. We have additional books on each subject should more study be advisable or necessary for you. Finally, the more you study, the better prepared you will be. This book is intended to be the last thing you study before you walk into the examination room. Prior study of relevant texts is also recommended. NLC publishes some of these in our Fundamental Series. Knowledge and good sense are important factors in passing your exam. Good luck also helps. So now study this Passbook, absorb the material contained within and take that knowledge into the examination. Then do your best to pass that exam.

EXAMINATION SECTION

EXAMINATION SECTION
TEST 1

DIRECTIONS: Each question or incomplete statement is followed by several suggested answers or completions. Select the one that BEST answers the question or completes the statement. *PRINT THE LETTER OF THE CORRECT ANSWER IN THE SPACE AT THE RIGHT.*

1. The vibration damper on an auto engine is fastened to the   1.____

    A. camshaft   B. flywheel
    C. crankshaft   D. driveshaft

2. MOST small gas engines use a(n) _____ ignition system.   2.____

    A. magneto   B. transistorized
    C. battery   D. induction

3. Carburetor icing occurs MOST often   3.____

    A. on humid, hot days
    B. when an engine is overheated
    C. on cool, damp days
    D. when an engine is run for long periods at idle speed

4. The function of the float in a carburetor is to   4.____

    A. close the needle valve
    B. control flow of gas into pump circuit
    C. operate choke circuit when engine is cold
    D. bleed off gasoline from primary tubes

5. To improve stability when cornering, manufacturers add a device to cars called a   5.____

    A. control arm   B. stabilizer bar
    C. constant velocity joint D. Pitman arm

6. Adjustment of the tie rods on a car will affect   6.____

    A. camber   B. king pin inclination
    C. caster   D. toe-in

7. A restriction in the exhaust system is indicated on a vacuum gauge by a   7.____

    A. steady needle
    B. low reading
    C. gradual decrease in reading
    D. fast fluctuating needle

8. Disc brakes on a car have a distinct advantage over conventional drum brakes in that they   8.____

    A. fade less when hot
    B. are cheaper to manufacture
    C. are easier to service
    D. require less pedal pressure to apply

1

9. In a diesel engine, the fuel is ignited by the

   A. spark plug
   B. injector plug
   C. heat of compression
   D. magneto

10. Engine timing is GENERALLY set by using a

    A. torque wrench
    B. dividing head
    C. strobe light
    D. centrifugal mechanism

11. If an engine is operated for long periods of time at part throttle opening, the

    A. spark plugs will become covered with carbon
    B. carburetor will become clogged
    C. fuel filter will accumulate more water
    D. points will blacken

12. Leaking intake valve guides will cause

    A. excessive oil consumption
    B. overheating
    C. valves to act sluggishly
    D. valve seats to burn

13. Flooding of a carburetor is GENERALLY caused by

    A. loose bolts holding carburetor to manifold
    B. air leaks in float bowl
    C. loose jets in carburetor body
    D. stuck float needle valve

14. On many cars, the fuel pump is combined with the

    A. vacuum pump
    B. power steering pump
    C. generator
    D. power brake booster

15. Carbon fouling of a spark plug is an indication of

    A. excessive oil burning
    B. too rich a mixture
    C. poor grade of gasoline
    D. plug misfiring

16. If tests show that generator output is excessive even after the F terminal has been disconnected, the trouble may be traced to

    A. the regulator
    B. the generator
    C. poor ground
    D. discharged battery

17. An automobile alternator converts alternating current to direct current by means of

    A. silicon diodes
    B. a current regulator
    C. a solenoid coil
    D. a magnetic shunt circuit

18. Hard starting is very often caused by

    A. a faulty condenser
    B. poor grade of gasoline
    C. improper grade of oil
    D. improper choke operation

19. A car with a history of *burned-points* would PROBABLY indicate

    A. improper gap setting
    B. improper condenser
    C. too high a setting of the voltage regulator
    D. incorrect dwell angle

20. When it is necessary to recondition brake drums, the MAXIMUM allowable amount of oversize is _____ inches.

    A. .025   B. .030   C. .040   D. .060

KEY (CORRECT ANSWERS)

1.	C	11.	A
2.	A	12.	A
3.	C	13.	D
4.	A	14.	A
5.	B	15.	B
6.	D	16.	B
7.	C	17.	A
8.	A	18.	D
9.	C	19.	C
10.	C	20.	D

TEST 2

DIRECTIONS: Each question or incomplete statement is followed by several suggested answers or completions. Select the one that BEST answers the question or completes the statement. *PRINT THE LETTER OF THE CORRECT ANSWER IN THE SPACE AT THE RIGHT.*

1. The amount of air-fuel mixture taken into the cylinder on the intake stroke is a measure of the engine's

    A. thermal efficiency
    B. volumetric efficiency
    C. rated horsepower
    D. mechanical efficiency

    1._____

2. Welch plugs are installed on engines to provide

    A. a means of removing the sand after the engine is cast
    B. inspection of the water jackets
    C. a means of cleaning the cooling system more effectively
    D. a means of draining the cooling system more quickly

    2._____

3. The two-cycle engine produces a power stroke with every _____ of the crankshaft.

    A. one-half revolution
    B. revolution
    C. two revolutions
    D. four revolutions

    3._____

4. Pre-ignition may be caused by

    A. carbon deposits
    B. a stuck valve
    C. an inoperative choke
    D. a broken ignition wire

    4._____

5. The size of an outboard motor propeller is ALWAYS given in

    A. degrees of thrust
    B. diameter and pitch
    C. circumference and number of blades
    D. diametral pitch

    5._____

6. Closed crankcase ventilation systems are used to

    A. get more power out of the engine
    B. reduce oil consumption
    C. increase the efficiency of the engine
    D. aid in prevention of air contamination

    6._____

7. The angular motion about the vertical axis of an aircraft or space craft is known as

    A. yaw   B. pitch   C. roll   D. bank

    7._____

8. The carburetor circuit that maintains a constant level of fuel in the float bowl is the _____ circuit.

    A. fuel
    B. accelerating pump
    C. float
    D. choke

    8._____

9. A jet engine combustion chamber liner is cooled by

    A. liquid coolants
    B. air streams
    C. heat exchangers
    D. convectors

    9._____

10. Regenerative gas turbine engines have been successfully developed for use on   10.____

    A. automobiles   B. motorcycles
    C. helicopters   D. tractors

11. Power impulses from the engine are *smoothed out* by the   11.____

    A. camshaft   B. clutch
    C. crankshaft   D. flywheel

12. The service ratings M S, S E, and S G refers to   12.____

    A. automotive fuels   B. automotive sealers
    C. motor oils   D. automotive greases

13. The intake and exhaust openings on a two-stroke cycle engine are known as   13.____

    A. vents   B. manifolds   C. scoops   D. ports

14. Ball-joint type front suspension eliminates   14.____

    A. the conventional kingpin
    B. the need for front-end alignment
    C. caster and camber adjustments
    D. the need for the usual tie-rods

15. Gasoline CANNOT be used in a diesel because the   15.____

    A. viscosity of gasoline is too low
    B. gasoline would start to burn long before the piston reached the top of the stroke
    C. injectors could not force gasoline into the cylinders
    D. injection pumps would *seize up* due to lack of lubrication

16. On the compression stroke, the diesel engine compresses   16.____

    A. air   B. air fuel mixture
    C. diesel fuel   D. heated engine oil

17. The idle and low speed circuit in a carburetor is inoperative   17.____

    A. at speeds under 20 mph
    B. at speeds over 20 mph
    C. when the choke is closed
    D. when the choke is open

18. A generator should be polarized to prevent damage whenever   18.____

    A. an adjustment is made to the regulator
    B. a low charging condition exists
    C. a high charging condition exists
    D. the generator or regulator wires have been disconnected

19. Turbo-prop engines are more efficient than turbo-jet engines for aircraft flying   19.____

    A. short trips   B. long trips
    C. over 500 mph   D. at high altitudes

20. A blower or pump which forces air into cylinders at higher than atmospheric pressures is known as a   20.____

    A. dynamometer   B. tachometer
    C. supercharger   D. stroboscope

KEY (CORRECT ANSWERS)

1.	B	11.	D
2.	A	12.	C
3.	B	13.	D
4.	A	14.	A
5.	B	15.	B
6.	D	16.	A
7.	A	17.	B
8.	C	18.	D
9.	B	19.	A
10.	A	20.	C

TEST 3

DIRECTIONS: Each question or incomplete statement is followed by several suggested answers or completions. Select the one that BEST answers the question or completes the statement. *PRINT THE LETTER OF THE CORRECT ANSWER IN THE SPACE AT THE RIGHT.*

1. The fuel pump is actuated by the
   A. camshaft
   B. crankshaft
   C. fan belt
   D. engine vacuum

   1._____

2. A storage battery becomes sulfated when the
   A. battery is charged
   B. battery is discharged
   C. acid content in the electrolyte is high
   D. battery is overcharged

   2._____

3. The MOST common cause for excess tire wear on edges is
   A. poor braking habits
   B. overinflation
   C. underinflation
   D. excessive speed

   3._____

4. The CORRECT order of piston rings above the piston pin is
   A. compression - oil - compression - oil
   B. oil - oil - compression - compression
   C. oil - compression - oil - compression
   D. compression - compression - oil - oil

   4._____

5. The voltage in the secondary of the ignition coil may reach _____ volts.
   A. 5000   B. 10,000   C. 20,000   D. 30,000

   5._____

6. Burnt ignition points are GENERALLY the result of
   A. faulty condenser
   B. points open too far
   C. reverse battery polarity
   D. defective ignition coil

   6._____

7. The MOST reliable method of testing a storage battery is by using a
   A. 6-volt test lamp
   B. voltmeter
   C. hydrometer
   D. high rate discharge cell tester

   7._____

8. In a normal operating engine, the vacuum gauge will read
   A.   B. 8-11   C. B,   D. 17-21   E.

   8._____

9. All of the following have moving parts EXCEPT the _____ jet engine.
   A. pulse   B. turbo-   C. ram   D. astro-

   9._____

7

10. The speed necessary to escape the gravitational pull of the earth is _____ miles per hour.

    A. 8,000   B. 40,000   C. 16,000   D. 25,000

11. The rocket designed to carry a man into space is the

    A. Titan   B. Jupiter   C. Saturn   D. Thor

12. Of the following statements about the flywheel, the one that is NOT true is: It is

    A. joined to the camshaft
    B. joined with the clutch driver plate
    C. a storer of energy
    D. joined with the crankshaft

13. A radiator fan is MOST essential

    A. in warm weather   B. at low speeds
    C. at high speeds   D. when idling

14. Rockets differ MAINLY from jet engines in that they

    A. are more powerful
    B. carry their own oxygen with them
    C. rely on gases thrusting out of the rear of the engine
    D. are heavier

15. For MAXIMUM power, the spark plug is timed to fire when the piston reaches

    A. top dead center   B. after top dead center
    C. before top dead center   D. a neutral position

16. Engine timing may be set MOST accurately with a

    A. dwell meter   B. vacuum gauge
    C. neon timing light   D. multimeter

17. The color around the electrodes of spark plugs which indicates normal wear is

    A. black   B. white to yellow
    C. brown   D. blue

18. On some late models of distributors, the cam angle is set with

    A. the cap left on
    B. the cap taken off
    C. a rotation of the rotor
    D. the removal of the distributor to a test bench

19. A soft brake is GENERALLY the result of

    A. grease on the brake lining
    B. air in the lines
    C. insufficient fluid
    D. poor brake adjustment

20. Toe-in is controlled by adjusting the

    A. tie rod
    B. spindle downward
    C. king pin angle
    D. steering knuckle

KEY (CORRECT ANSWERS)

1.	A	11.	C
2.	B	12.	A
3.	C	13.	D
4.	B	14.	B
5.	C	15.	C
6.	A	16.	A
7.	D	17.	B
8.	B	18.	A
9.	C	19.	B
10.	D	20.	A

TEST 4

DIRECTIONS: Each question or incomplete statement is followed by several suggested answers or completions. Select the one that BEST answers the question or completes the statement. *PRINT THE LETTER OF THE CORRECT ANSWER IN THE SPACE AT THE RIGHT.*

1. The MAIN reason car manufacturers use a pressurized cooling system is that it

   A. simplifies the cooling system
   B. permits any type of anti-freeze to be used
   C. permits the engine to run at high temperatures without evaporation of the coolant
   D. permits less maintenance

1.____

2. Testing an outboard motor in a test barrel requires

   A. reduced speed
   B. a test wheel
   C. an external fuel supply
   D. a constant source of cool water

2.____

3. On two-cycle engines, oil changes are NOT necessary because

   A. the sealed bearings they are equipped With require no lubrication
   B. the oil is generally mixed with the fuel
   C. the non-leaded gas which they require has lubricating qualities of its own
   D. modern detergent oils retain their lubricating qualities indefinitely .

3.____

4. The governor that many small one-cylinder gasoline engines use to maintain a constant speed under varying loads is *generally* connected to the

   A. throttle   B. flywheel
   C. choke   D. intake valve or reed

4.____

5. Fuel is supplied to the carburetor on power lawn mowers by means of

   A. a fuel pump   B. vacuum
   C. intake reeds   D. gravity

5.____

6. Some jet engines are equipped with an afterburner; the purpose of this device is to

   A. provide extra power in emergencies
   B. reduce air pollution
   C. reduce the speed of the turbine itself
   D. reduce the overall size of the engine

6.____

7. Magneto Armature Air Gap refers to the space between the

   A. points and the magneto
   B. magneto coil and its armature
   C. points
   D. rotating flywheel and the coil-armature pole shoes

7.____

8. In a magneto ignition system, the primary current is supplied by means of

   A. a 6-volt battery supply
   B. a 1 1/2-volts battery supply
   C. a primary coil and a permanent magnet
   D. any D.C. source

9. In a standard hydraulic brake system, the brake pedal leverage is in the ratio of

   A. 10 to 1   B. 8 to 1   C. 5 to 1   D. 1 to 1

10. A quick test to determine the condition of a storage battery is to

    A. use a cadmium test
    B. inspect the level of the electrolyte
    C. observe its charging rate in the car
    D. use a high discharge tester

11. Cavitation is a condition which causes

    A. air to enter the cooling system
    B. a boat propeller to lose its *grip* on the water
    C. bubbles to form around a boat hull, thus preventing ice from forming
    D. spark plug fouling

12. If, during a tune-up, a vacuum gauge reading shows a slowly floating needle over a range of 4 or 5 points, it is an indication of

    A. a defective heat value   B. a normal operating condition
    C. a faulty carburetor adjustment   D. leaking cylinder rings

13. Dwell angle is an IMPORTANT factor to consider during a tune-up because it refers to

    A. degrees of rotation of the distributor cam during which the points remain open
    B. degrees of rotation of the distributor cam during which time the points remain closed
    C. the gap between the points
    D. the angle formed by the cam and the points

14. Pistons are cam-ground so as to produce

    A. a perfectly symmetrical cylinder
    B. a smooth surface
    C. pistons whose diameter is less at the pin bosses
    D. pistons whose diameter is greater at the pin bosses

15. Advertised horsepower ratings of automotive engines are almost always assumed to be *indicated horsepower*.
    These ratings are obtained by

    A. adding the brake horsepower to the friction horsepower
    B. using the SAE horsepower formula
    C. using a brake test
    D. formula only

16. During a tune-up, an electrical tachometer should be hooked up as follows: one lead to the ground, the other lead to the

    A. distributor side of the coil
    B. engine side of the coil
    C. number one spark plug
    D. ignition switch

16.____

17. When testing diodes from an alternator with a diode tester, a reading of two amperes *generally* indicates a(n) _____ diode.

    A. faulty   B. good   C. open   D. shorted

17.____

18. One of the MAIN disadvantages of the PCV system is that it causes

    A. corrosion on the precisely fitted engine parts
    B. excessive gasoline consumption
    C. some degree of engine overheating
    D. increased oil consumption

18.____

19. The average operating pressure of a conventional mechanical-type fuel pump is _____ pounds.

    A. 5   B. 8   C. 10   D. 12

19.____

20. Casing-head gasoline is an extremely volatile liquid obtained from

    A. low grade petroleum   B. natural gas
    C. selective cracking   D. Pennsylvania crude oil

20.____

KEY (CORRECT ANSWERS)

1.	C	11.	B
2.	B	12.	C
3.	B	13.	B
4.	A	14.	C
5.	D	15.	A
6.	A	16.	A
7.	D	17.	B
8.	C	18.	A
9.	B	19.	A
10.	D	20.	B

EXAMINATION SECTION
TEST 1

DIRECTIONS: Each question or incomplete statement is followed by several suggested answers or completions. Select the one that BEST answers the question or completes the statement. *PRINT THE LETTER OF THE CORRECT ANSWER IN THE SPACE AT THE RIGHT.*

1. Piston rings are used to
   A. keep the piston from wearing
   B. prevent leakage of gas into the crankcase
   C. keep the cylinder walls smooth
   D. reduce the friction between the cylinder walls and the piston

   1.____

2. By camber is meant the
   A. forward tilt of the king pin
   B. backward tilt of the king pin
   C. outward tilt of the front wheels from the vertical
   D. difference of the distance between the front wheels at the front and at the rear of the front wheels

   2.____

3. An engine develops more torque when the car is
   A. rounding a curve   B. going down a hill
   C. in low speed   D. in high speed

   3.____

4. When the brakes of a car squeak as they are applied, the PROBABLE cause is the fact that the brake
   A. linings are dry   B. linings are wet
   C. pedal is out of adjustment D. shoes are warped

   4.____

5. A compression test of all cylinders in an automobile engine is made PRIMARILY to
   A. check uniformity among the cylinders
   B. obtain the highest reading possible
   C. check on the specified compression ratio
   D. check the cylinder bore condition

   5.____

6. Valve springs are used to
   A. open the valves   B. keep the valves open
   C. open and close the valves D. close the valves

   6.____

7. A common cause of an over-rich carburetor mixture is a
   A. dirty air cleaner
   B. leaking intake valve in the fuel pump
   C. low float level in the carburetor
   D. late spark timing

   7.____

8. The pin that transmits power from the piston to the connecting rod is called the _____ pin.
   A. king
   B. wrist
   C. connecting rod
   D. taper

9. Spark plugs that foul because of excessive carbon formation produced by slow speed engine operation can be corrected by
   A. installing spark plugs of a higher heat range
   B. advancing the ignition timing
   C. lowering the carburetor fuel level
   D. adjusting the manifold heat control valve

10. In a six-cylinder engine, the cranks on the crankshaft are set apart _____ degrees.
    A. 30   B. 45   C. 120   D. 60

11. A carburetor that causes hard starting when the engine is hot may be corrected by
    A. the installation of an accelerator pump piston
    B. an anti-percolating valve
    C. installing a new high speed jet
    D. adjustment of the throttle valve set screw

12. A dragging of the brakes at one wheel may be caused by
    A. excessive grease on the lining
    B. a clogged brake line
    C. insufficient fluid in the master cylinder
    D. a leaking wheel cylinder

13. Toe-in of front wheels is necessary to
    A. offset the drag created by the caster angle
    B. compensate for the decrease in the king pin inclination
    C. produce easy recovery to a straight ahead position after turning a corner
    D. overcome the run-out due to the camber angle

14. A manifold heat control valve that is sticking in the *open* position will cause
    A. sluggish engine operation when cold
    B. hard starting when the engine is hot
    C. vapor lock
    D. a substantial increase in fuel consumption

15. A vacuum gauge shows a normal engine condition when
    A. the reading indicates a fluctuation between 15 and 17 inches of mercury
    B. there is a steady reading of 17 to 21 inches of mercury
    C. there is an intermittent reading of 16 to 18 inches of mercury
    D. there is a steady reading of 16 inches of mercury

16. A cam ground piston means that it
    A. is elliptical in shape
    B. uses no piston rings
    C. has no wrist pin
    D. has a complex head formation

17. Accurate spacing of the distributor points is accomplished with the use of a
    A. flat thickness gauge
    B. round thickness gauge
    C. syncroscope
    D. dial indicator

18. Hydraulic brake liquid leaking at the rubber boot at the end of a master cylinder USUALLY indicates
    A. a faulty check valve
    B. that the master cylinder has been overfilled
    C. leakage at the primary cup
    D. leakage at the master cylinder cup washer

19. Light detonation or spark knock that occurs when accelerating with a fully opened throttle on a hard pull indicates that
    A. the spark is too far advanced
    B. the spark is too far retarded
    C. the condition is normal
    D. a low grade of fuel is being used

20. Breaker points in service for some time may appear dull and gray upon inspection. This condition is
    A. due to a high battery voltage
    B. due to improper condenser capacity
    C. a normal condition
    D. due to a high resistance in the primary circuit

21. When a conventional automobile transmission is in neutral position, with the clutch engaged and the engine running,
    A. both the countershaft and the clutch shaft are turning
    B. only the countershaft is turning
    C. only the clutch shaft is turning
    D. only the reverse idler shaft is turning

22. The condenser in the electrical system of an automobile is used to
    A. increase the spark at the distributor points
    B. retard the ignition timing
    C. reduce arcing at the breaker points
    D. complete the primary circuit

23. Positive camber in the front wheels tends to
    A. overcome the effect of *toe-in*
    B. overcome the effect of *toe-out*
    C. overcome the effect of caster
    D. center the weight of the vehicle on the large inner wheel cearing

24. Hypoid rear ends should be lubricated with a(n)
    A. aluminum soap grease
    B. fibrous grease
    C. low pressure lubricant
    D. extreme pressure lubricant

25. The MAIN advantage of hydraulic brake systems is that they
    A. do not wear out the linings as rapidly as mechanical brakes do
    B. apply uniform pressure to each set of wheel brakes
    C. stop the automobile more quickly
    D. do not require adjustment

26. The purpose of an overdrive unit on automobile is to
    A. increase the speed of an engine in relation to the speed of the wheels
    B. simplify shifting
    C. increase the speed of the wheels in relation to the speed of the engine
    D. aid in braking the speed of the car when descending hills

27. The S.A.E. number of a lubricant indicates its
    A. tar content   B. flash point
    C. viscosity   D. acid content

28. *Hot, cold,* or *standard* spark plugs are distinguished by the
    A. shape and length of the lower porcelain insulator
    B. overall length of the plug
    C. diameter of the shell
    D. thickness of the shell

29. The amount of fuel mixture that can be drawn into a cylinder depends upon the
    A. displacement of the piston   B. combustion chamber area
    C. spark timing   D. speed of the fuel pump

30. To adjust the valves of an automobile engine, it is necessary to have the piston on
    A. bottom dead center
    B. top dead center
    C. intake stroke
    D. top dead center compression stroke

31. The backing plate on all automobiles is used PRIMARILY to
    A. retain the axle in the housing
    B. keep water from entering the brake mechanism
    C. provide a support for the brake shoes
    D. aid in stopping the automobile

32. The Hotchkiss type of rear-end drive uses
    A. two radius rods, sometimes attached to the front ends of the rear housing and to the upper face of the car's frame
    B. the two rear springs to absorb the rear-end torque and to transmit the driving thrust to the frame of the car
    C. two angle irons shaped like the letter *V*, reinforced with a cross rod
    D. a metal casing around the driveshaft

33. The camshaft of a four-stroke cycle engine rotates at 33.____
    A. crankshaft speed   B. one-half crankshaft speed
    C. one-quarter crankshaft speed   D. twice crankshaft speed

34. Looking in the direction in which a current flow through a conductor, the 34.____
    magnetic field surrounding it always travels in a(n) _____ direction.
    A. alternating   B. anti-clockwise
    C. southerly   D. clockwise

35. Contact point spring pressure should be set at _____ ounces 35.____
    A. 6 to 10   B. 17 to 21   C. 31 to 35   D. 36 to 40

36. The resistance of a suppressor may be measured by a(n) 36.____
    A. voltmeter   B. ohmmeter
    C. watt meter   D. inductance meter

37. The capacity of a condenser is generally measured in 37.____
    A. microfarads   B. farads   C. milliamps   D. ohms

38. Breaker points of a six cylinder engine should be set at 38.____
    A. .018   B. .0018   C. .180   D. 1.80

39. A fuse is placed in the lighting circuit to prevent 39.____
    A. short circuit   B. horn from blowing
    C. damage to wiring   D. overload of generator

40. The voltage of a battery is determined by 40.____
    A. the number of plates in each cell
    B. adding a stronger acid solution to the electrolyte
    C. connecting more cells in parallel
    D. connecting more cells in series

41. The blood vessels that carry blood toward the heart are the 41.____
    A. arteries   B. capillaries   C. corpuscles   D. veins

42. If an artery has been cut, you could tell by the 42.____
    A. quick clotting of the blood   B. Rh factor of the blood
    C. slow, steady flow of blood   D. spurting of the blood

43. The BEST material to be used directly over a wound or burn is 43.____
    A. absorbent cotton   B. adhesive tape
    C. sterile gauze   D. a tourniquet

44. Aromatic spirits of ammonia is used as a(n) 44.____
    A. antidote for arsenic poisoning   B. stimulant
    C. sedative drug   D. sterilizing solution

45. A compound fracture is one in which 45._____
    A. broken bones protrude through the skin
    B. bones are broken and shattered
    C. a large bone and its adjoining smaller bones are broken
    D. two or more bones are broken

Questions 46-50.

DIRECTIONS: Each of Questions 46 through 50 consists of a group of four words. Examine each group carefully, then in the space at the right print the letter
A if only one word in the group is spelled correctly
B if two words in the group are spelled correctly
C if three words in the group are spelled correctly
D if all four words in the group are spelled correctly

46. Wendsday, particular, similar, hunderd 46._____

47. realize, judgment, opportunities, consistent 47._____

48. equel, principle, assistense, commitee 48._____

49. simultaneous, privilege, advise, ocassionaly 49._____

50. necissery, official, Febuary, distence

KEY (CORRECT ANSWERS)

1. B	11. B	21. A	31. C	41. D
2. C	12. B	22. C	32. B	42. D
3. C	13. D	23. D	33. B	43. C
4. D	14. A	24. D	34. D	44. B
5. A	15. B	25. B	35. B	45. A
6. D	16. A	26. C	36. B	46. B
7. A	17. D	27. C	37. A	47. D
8. B	18. D	28. A	38. A	48. A
9. A	19. C	29. A	39. C	49. C
10. C	20. C	30. D	40. D	50. A

TEST 2

DIRECTIONS: Each question consists of a statement. You are to indicate whether the statement is TRUE (T) or FALSE (F). *PRINT THE LETTER OF THE CORRECT ANSWER IN THE SPACE AT THE RIGHT.*

1. The starting of an engine is NOT affected by a sticking automatic choke. 1.____

2. To aid the starting of an overchoked engine, it is necessary to crank the engine with the throttle wide open to help clear the cylinders of raw gasoline. 2.____

3. The oil pressure gauge indicates the quantity of oil in the crankcase. 3.____

4. A lighter grade of oil should be used during cold weather driving. 4.____

5. The purpose of the cooling fan is to help dissipate the heat from the cylinder block. 5.____

6. The generator is a device which converts mechanical energy into electrical energy. 6.____

7. A shunt generator without a voltage regulator will not tend to increase the voltage output with the increase in the engine speed. 7.____

8. The output of a third brush generator is increased by moving the third brush away from the main brush. 8.____

9. The cut-out relay prevents the battery from discharging through the generator when the engine is stopped. 9.____

10. The coil in an ignition system is used to build up a high voltage in the primary circuit. 10.____

11. To check the condition of a storage batter, it is only necessary to check the specific gravity of the acid in the storage battery. 11.____

12. A specific gravity reading of 1.100 indicates a battery in full charge condition. 12.____

13. When the battery acid reading varies between the cells of a storage battery, it is only necessary to add stronger acid to the weak cells. 13.____

14. Distributor rotor shafts always rotate in a clockwise direction. 14.____

15. A good spark at the spark plug depends entirely on the charge condition of the storage battery. 15.____

16. The condenser helps to quench the spark at the breaker points. 16.____

17. Breaker points will burn away rapidly if the cam angle is too great. 17.____

18. If the lights dim considerably when the starting motor is operated, this indicates a faulty ground connection. 18.____

19. Increasing temperatures cause oil to gain body and lose fluidity, while decreasing temperatures cause oil to lose body and gain fluidity. 19.____

20. In a splash lubricating system, the oil is pumped under pressure to all working parts of the engine. 20.____

21. An over-rich carburetor mixture is indicated by a white smoke emitted from the exhaust pipe. 21.____

22. When an engine stalls after a violent braking of the vehicle, it indicates that the carburetor idling mixture is too lean. 22.____

23. High speed duel supply depends entirely on the idling jet in the carburetor. 23.____

24. The accelerator pump injects a supply of gasoline to the manifold when the throttle is opened suddenly. 24.____

25. To pressure flush a radiator, it is proper to exert a pressure at the top of the core to force the clogged material out of the bottom of the core. 25.____

26. An engine water thermostat is provided to restrict water circulation when the engine is cold. 26.____

27. Corrosion of the radiator and parts of the cooling system may be caused by exhaust gas leaking into the cooling system through a defective cylinder head gasket. 27.____

28. An L-head type of engine is one in which the intake valves are located on one side of the engine block and the exhaust valves are located on the other side of the engine block. 28.____

29. A worn valve guide will cause excessive oil consumption. 29.____

30. Counterweights on crankshafts are provided to compensate for the weight of the flywheel. 30.____

31. Worn main bearings will produce a typical crankshaft knock that is especially noticeable when the engine is under a hard pull. 31.____

32. An oil wiper ring on a piston is a device that insures proper lubrication to the cylinder walls. 32.____

33. The order in which the events of a four-stroke cycle occur is: 1 – compression, 2 – intake, 3 – power, 4 – exhaust. 33.____

34. Fuels for gasoline engines are rated according to octane number, those having the higher octane rating are those having the GREATEST tendency to knock. 34.____

35. An efficient combustible mixture for a gasoline engine is one part of gasoline to fifteen parts of air by volume. 35.____

36. A loose piston pin will indicate itself by a double knock MOSTLY noticeable during idling. 36.____

37. The operation of a clutch is based on the frictional contact between two smooth metallic surfaces and the facings riveted to the friction disk. 37.____

38. A slipping clutch may be caused by the lack of free clutch pedal action. 38.____

39. Hydraulic transmissions are operated by the vacuum produced in the engine intake manifold. 39.____

40. A chattering clutch may be caused by oil or gum on the pressure plate, friction disk, or flywheel facing. 40.____

41. A dragging clutch may be caused by a warped or distorted pressure plate. 41.____

42. Syncro mesh devices are designed to cause gear that are rotating and about to be meshed to rotate at the same speeds so that meshing can take place easily. 42.____

43. In constant mesh type transmissions, the gears are moved to become engaged or disengaged according to the need. 43.____

44. The vacuum or power gear shift uses intake manifold vacuum to provide the needed power to shift gears. 44.____

45. The overdrive unit reduces engine speed for high car speeds, providing more economical operation and less engine wear per car mile. 45.____

46. Hard gear shifting may be caused by sliding gears being tight on the splined shaft. 46.____

47. The proper shaft universal joints are provided to allow for the difference in shaft positions when the wheels ride over a bump. 47.____

48. A differential is required to compensate for the difference in distances the rear wheels travel when the car rounds a turn. 48.____

49. In the semi-floating type of rear axle, the wheel end of the axle shaft is supported by a bearing in the axle housing. 49.____

50. A leaf spring has a slower rate of vibration than a coil spring, thereby giving a much easier ride. 50.____

KEY (CORRECT ANSWERS)

1.	F	11.	F	21.	F	31.	T	41.	T
2.	T	12.	F	22.	T	32.	F	42.	T
3.	F	13.	F	23.	F	33.	F	43.	F
4.	T	14.	F	24.	T	34.	F	44.	T
5.	T	15.	F	25.	F	35.	F	45.	T
6.	T	16.	T	26.	T	36.	T	46.	T
7.	F	17.	T	27.	T	37.	T	47.	T
8.	F	18.	F	28.	F	38.	T	48.	T
9.	T	19.	F	29.	T	39.	F	49.	T
10.	F	20.	F	30.	F	40.	T	50.	F

TEST 3

DIRECTIONS: Each question consists of a statement. You are to indicate whether the statement is TRUE (T) or FALSE (F). *PRINT THE LETTER OF THE CORRECT ANSWER IN THE SPACE AT THE RIGHT.*

1. A weak front spring of the leaf type may cause a change in the caster effect. 1._____

2. Shock absorbers are provided to overcome the violent rebound action after a spring has been compressed. 2._____

3. The hydraulic type of shock absorber depends upon the difference of air pressure within the unit for its efficient operation. 3._____

4. Caster effect is put into a front axle by tilting the upper parts of the king pin towards the front of the car. 4._____

5. Excessive caster effect will cause the wheels to shimmy. 5._____

6. On modern vehicles, the camber effect is kept at a minimum due to the king pin inclination. 6._____

7. Excessive camber may cause tire wear at the outer edge of the tire. 7._____

8. Scuffing of the tire surface may be caused by a bent steering arm. 8._____

9. The pitman arm is the connecting link between the steering gear assembly and the drag link. 9._____

10. The reach rod connects the front wheels with the steering column. 10._____

11. Steering arms must be positioned to give proper toe-in when the car is on a turn. 11._____

12. If a car persistently pulls to one side, this may be caused by low or uneven tire pressures. 12._____

13. Steering gears are provided with adjustments to eliminate end play in the cross shaft and worm and wheel contact. 13._____

14. A properly adjusted steering gear will be indicated by a slight drag at the center position and free action at the extreme end positions. 14._____

15. When checking for caster, camber, or toe-in, it is necessary to have the car in a level position and the tires inflated to the proper pressures. 15._____

16. The effectiveness of hydraulic brakes is based upon the principle that hydraulic pressure is exerted equally in all directions in a liquid under pressure. 16._____

17. Noisy or squealing brakes may be caused by loose linings or rivets that touch the brake drum. 17._____

18. When all brakes drag on a car equipped with a hydraulic system, this condition may be caused by a clogged filler vent on the master cylinder. 18._____

19. Air in the hydraulic brake lines indicates the necessity for bleeding the entire brake system. 19._____

20. Piston displacement is the volume that the piston displaces as it moves from top dead center to bottom dead center position. 20._____

21. The stroke of an engine is the distance the piston travels from top dead center to bottom dead center 21._____

22. Low pressure in a full force lubrication system may indicate loose bearings. 22._____

23. A cracked distributor cap may cause a miss in the engine. 23._____

24. The S.A.E. number of lubricating oils indicates the degree of viscosity of the oil. 24._____

25. Vapor lock will NOT affect the running of an engine. 25._____

26. Late spark timing will cause an engine to overheat. 26._____

27. Excessive pressure in air brake systems may be caused by sticking relief valves. 27._____

28. A magneto depends upon a battery for a current to operate the breaker system. 28._____

29. The intensity of a spark produced by a magneto depends upon the speed of the magneto armature. 29._____

30. The camshaft of an engine rotates at one-half the speed of the crankshaft. 30._____

31. A battery that is badly sulphated may be corrected by placing the battery on a low charge for a long period of time. 31._____

32. A voltage regulator controls the voltage output of the battery. 32._____

33. Rebound clips on leaf springs are provided to prevent the spring from shifting on the spring saddle. 33._____

34. The fuel pump that delivers gasoline to the carburetor does so under pressure. 34._____

35. A high float level in the carburetor may cause an over-rich operating condition. 35.____

36. Crankcase ventilation is provided to help carry off the vapors of water and gasoline when the engine reaches operating temperature. 36.____

37. The pressure cap allows circulation of water in the cooling system at higher temperatures without boiling. 37.____

38. Excessive fuel consumption may be caused by underinflated tires. 38.____

39. Accelerator pump linkage control must be adjusted for winter and for summer driving. 39.____

40. Excessive oil consumption may be caused by a broken oil seal at the rear main bearing. 40.____

41. If a battery is allowed to stand for a long period of time, it will slowly self-discharge. 41.____

42. If the battery requires a considerable amount of water, it indicates that the charge rate is too low. 42.____

43. It is advisable to coat the battery terminals with petroleum jelly to prevent corrosion. 43.____

44. A low or unsteady output from a generator may be caused by a round, dirty, or worn commutator. 44.____

45. Valve tappet noise may be caused by excessive clearance between the valve stem and the valve guide. 45.____

46. A slipping clutch is caused by excessive pressure of the pressure springs. 46.____

47. The transmission interlocking device is provided to prevent the shifting of more than one gear at a time. 47.____

48. High speed driving will not wear tires more than slow speed driving. 48.____

49. High speed driving on hot pavements will cause a rise in pressure in the tire. 49.____

50. Spark plug gaps must be varied according to the compression ratio of the engine. 50.____

KEY (CORRECT ANSWERS)

1. T	11. F	21. T	31. T	41. T
2. T	12. T	22. T	32. F	42. F
3. F	13. T	23. T	33. F	43. T
4. F	14. T	24. T	34. T	44. T
5. T	15. T	25. F	35. T	45. F
6. T	16. T	26. T	36. T	46. F
7. T	17. T	27. T	37. T	47. T
8. T	18. T	28. F	38. T	48. F
9. T	19. T	29. T	39. T	49. T
10. F	20. T	30. T	40. T	50. F

EXAMINATION SECTION
TEST 1

DIRECTIONS: Each question or incomplete statement is followed by several suggested answers or completions. Select the one that BEST answers the question or completes the statement. *PRINT THE LETTER OF THE CORRECT ANSWER IN THE SPACE AT THE RIGHT.*

1. If a carburetor drips continually, the MOST likely cause is a   1.____
   A. loose Venturi tube
   B. needle valve not seating
   C. loose idle set screw
   D. float set too low

2. The part used to control the ratio of air and gasoline in a truck engine is the   2.____
   A. bogie   B. filter   C. carburetor   D. pump

3. During cranking, all electrical energy is supplied by the   3.____
   A. alternator   B. battery   C. generator   D. engine

4. A device for storing electric charges is known as a(n)   4.____
   A. commutator   B. condenser   C. capacitance   D. exciter

5. Hydraulic brake fluid is a mixture of _____ and _____.   5.____
   A. kerosene; engine oil
   B. mineral oil; denatured alcohol
   C. castor oil; denatured alcohol
   D. ethelene glycol; mineral oil

6. When you are servicing the air brake chambers located at each wheel, the bolts and nuts holding the diaphragm plates should be tightened   6.____
   A. more tightly on the pressure plate than on the non-pressure plate
   B. more tightly on the non-pressure plate than on the pressure plate
   C. with only sufficient pressure to insure an air-tight seal
   D. with as much pressure as possible

7. The temperature gauge indicates the temperature of the   7.____
   A. air surrounding the engine
   B. water surrounding the cylinders
   C. oil in the crankcase
   D. pistons

8. Air drawn into the cooling system through the pump or hoses causes   8.____
   A. better cooling of the water
   B. the water to stop circulating
   C. a boost in the circulation
   D. rusting of the cylinder block

9. Diesel fuel filter elements on an International Harvester or Allis-Chalmers tractor are USUALLY serviced when too dirt for continued use by   9.____
   A. washing in kerosene
   B. steam cleaning
   C. washing in carbon tetrachloride
   D. oiling

10. To find out if a cylinder of a diesel engine is firing, it is necessary to
    A. remove the fuel pump
    B. disconnect the vent valve
    C. remove the vent valve
    D. prime the injection pump

11. In diesel engines, piston rings are held against the side of the cylinder PRIMARILY by
    A. gas pressure behind the ring
    B. thermal expansion of the ring
    C. an oil wedge behind the ring
    D. spring forces within the ring itself

12. In addition to lighter weight, the PRINCIPAL advantage of aluminum alloy pistons in diesel engines is that
    A. piston rings have less tendency to collect sludge and stick
    B. they have a much higher heat transfer rate than cast iron pistons
    C. they expand less under heat and thus reduce liner wear
    D. area for area, they are stronger than cast iron

13. All the refrigerant now used for automotive air conditioners is R
    A. 10 B. 12 C. 18 D. 22

14. When the right front wheel is turned 20° to the left, the left front wheel should turn APPROXIMATELY _____ degrees.
    A. 16 B. 18 C. 20 D. 24

15. In placing a new tire and a well-worn tire on dual wheels, it is BEST to place
    A. the new tire on the inside
    B. the worn tire on the inside
    C. either tire on the inside; it makes no difference
    D. the tires separately

16. The color of iron at welding heat is USUALLY a
    A. creamy white B. dull yellow C. light yellow D. light red

17. The _____ raring method measures the amount of current a battery can supply steadily for 20 hours, with no cell falling below 1.75 volts.
    A. cold-cranking
    B. reserve-capacity
    C. watts
    D. ampere-hour

18. In an automotive gasoline engine, the camshaft is used PRIMARILY to
    A. drive the transmission
    B. operate the valve lifters
    C. change the reciprocating motion of the pistons to rotary motion
    D. operate the choke mechanism

19. The PRIMARY function of the thermostat in the cooling system of an automobile engine is to
    A. control the operating temperature of the engine
    B. keep the operating temperature of the engine as low as possible
    C. provide the proper amount of heat for the heater
    D. retain engine heat when the engine gets hot

20. The PRIMARY purpose of the condenser in the ignition circuit of a gasoline engine is to
    A. boost the ignition voltage
    B. rectify the ignition voltage
    C. adjust the coil voltage
    D. reducing arcing of the distributor breaker points

20.____

21. The PRIMARY purpose of the differential in the rear drive train of an automotive vehicle is to allow each of the rear wheels to
    A. rotate at different speeds   B. go in reverse
    C. rotate with maximum torque   D. absorb road shocks

21.____

22. Of the following, the BEST tool to use for securely tightening a one-inch standard hexagonal nut is a(n)
    A. monkey wrench   B. open-end wrench
    C. Stillson wrench   D. pair of heavy duty pliers

22.____

23. The purpose of the ignition coil in a gasoline engine is PRIMARILY to
    A. smooth the voltage   B. raise the voltage
    C. raise the current   D. smooth the current

23.____

24. Vapor lock in a vehicle with a gasoline engine is caused by excessive heat. To prevent vapor lock, it may be necessary to relocate
    A. the ignition system B. the cooling system
    C. the starter motor   D. a part of the fuel line

24.____

25. It is important to use safety shoes PRIMARILY to guard the feet against
    A. tripping hazards   B. heavy falling objects
    C. shock hazards   D. mud and dirt

25.____

KEY (CORRECT ANSWERS)

1.	B		11.	D
2.	C		12.	C
3.	B		13.	B
4.	B		14.	D
5.	C		15.	D
6.	C		16.	A
7.	B		17.	B
8.	D		18.	B
9.	A		19.	A
10.	B		20.	D

21. A
22. B
23. B
24. D
25. B

TEST 2

DIRECTIONS: Each question or incomplete statement is followed by several suggested answers or completions. Select the one that BEST answers the question or completes the statement. *PRINT THE LETTER OF THE CORRECT ANSWER IN THE SPACE AT THE RIGHT.*

1. Which of the following is a PROBABLE result of a malfunctioning PCV valve? 1.____
   A. High fuel tank pressure
   B. Improper idling
   C. Noisy engine valves
   D. High fuel consumption

2. When a car goes into overdrive, the _____ gear is held stationary. 2.____
   A. pinion   B. ring   C. sun   D. planetary

3. A puller is NOT commonly used to remove or install 3.____
   A. valves   B. gears   C. pulleys   D. bearings

4. An engine turbocharger draws its energy from 4.____
   A. ignition spark
   B. engine fan airflow
   C. cylinder combustion
   D. hot exhaust gases

5. A four-gas automotive emissions analyzer will NOT measure the presence of 5.____
   A. HC   B. CO   C. CO_2 D. NO

6. An automotive cylinder head is attached to the 6.____
   A. bearing saddle
   B. pan rail
   C. boss
   D. block deck

7. Which of the following is a DISADVANTAGE associated with a magnetic reluctance crankshaft position sensor that is used in a microprocessor-based control/diagnostic system? 7.____
   A. Inability to directly measure crankshaft position
   B. Inability to exploit flywheel rotation
   C. Requires additional installation of a harmonic damper
   D. Inability to set engine timing statically

8. Which valve train component CANNOT be used on overhead cam engines? 8.____
   A. Finger follower
   B. Bucket follower
   C. Tappet
   D. Rocker arm

9. Which of the following would likely be indicated by uneven firing voltages that are displayed on an oscilloscope? 9.____
   A. Worn plug electrodes
   B. Condenser failure
   C. Arcing contact points
   D. Point contact failure

10. Power steering systems typically use each of the following types of pumps EXCEPT 10.____
    A. vane   B. diaphragm   C. roller   D. slipper

11. Most exhaust gas analyzers used in emission control maintenance indicate the percentage of _____ in the exhaust.
    A. HC   B. CO   C. NO   D. CO_2

12. What is the term for the portion of a cam that has a constant diameter, and does not produce lift as it rotates?
    A. Offset   B. Nose circle   C. Flank circle   D. Radial circle

13. In a microprocessor-based control/diagnostic system, which type of sensor uses the compound zirconia oxide?
    A. MAP
    B. Throttle angle
    C. EGO
    D. Knock

14. Which measuring device is MAINLY used to find open circuits and excessive resistance by imposing a bypass on a portion of the existing circuit?
    A. Digital multimeter
    B. Jumper wires
    C. Test light
    D. Continuity tester

15. If a car engine is operating at 1500 rpm, at what speed (rpm) is the distributor running?
    A. 750   B. 1500   C. 3000   D. 4500

16. Throttle body fuel injection refers to
    A. the insertion of fuel below the throttle plate
    B. unregulated fuel flow
    C. a continuous flow fuel injection
    D. a form of fuel metering actuator used in microprocessor-based control/diagnostic systems

17. Which of the following conditions in the valve train is NOT consistent with the *open valve* position in engine operation?
    A. Upward oil flow
    B. Plunger extended
    C. Slight leakage between plunger and body
    D. Ball check valve closed

18. What is the term for projections on a plate or disc that interlock in hub or drum slots?
    A. Drive lugs
    B. Toe cams
    C. Axial teeth
    D. Plate threads

19. Which of the following conditions is a POSSIBLE result of evaporation control system failure?
    A. Collapsed fuel tank
    B. High fuel tank pressure
    C. Improper idle
    D. Vapor low from air cleaner

20. Each of the following is a problem commonly associated with improper casting angles EXCEPT
    A. pulling to one side
    B. hard steering
    C. high speed instability
    D. rapid tire wear

    20._____

21. In a microprocessor-based control/diagnostic system, which type of crankshaft position sensor is located in the distributor?
    A. Optical
    B. Ignition timing
    C. Hall-effect
    D. Magnetic reluctance

    21._____

22. When using a short finder to trace a short circuit, which of the following steps should be performed FIRST?
    A. Turn on all switches in a series with the circuit being tested
    B. Move the short finder meter along circuit wiring
    C. Remove the blown fuse while leaving the battery connected
    D. Connect the pulse unit of short finder across the fuse terminals

    22._____

23. In a fuel injection system, which type of pump is used PRIMARILY as a transfer pump?
    A. Rotary
    B. Diaphragm
    C. Turbine
    D. Roller

    23._____

24. What type of electrical connectors are used to permanently join two stripped wire ends?
    A. Crimp
    B. Flat blade
    C. Butt
    D. Snap-splice

    24._____

25. Discharges from the _____ appear as high voltage surges on an oscilloscope tester.
    A. distributor
    B. contact points
    C. coil high-tension terminal
    D. battery

    25._____

KEY (CORRECT ANSWERS)

1.	B	11.	B
2.	C	12.	C
3.	A	13.	C
4.	D	14.	B
5.	D	15.	A
6.	D	16.	D
7.	D	17.	B
8.	C	18.	A
9.	A	19.	D
10.	B	20.	D

21. C
22. C
23. B
24. C
25. C

EXAMINATION SECTION
TEST 1

DIRECTIONS: Each question or incomplete statement is followed by several suggested answers or completions. Select the one that BEST answers the question or completes the statement. *PRINT THE LETTER OF THE CORRECT ANSWER IN THE SPACE AT THE RIGHT.*

1. If a gasoline engine cylinder is excessively worn, it will be found that the wear is practically always GREATEST
   A. at the top of the ring travel
   B. at the middle of the ring travel
   C. at the lowest ring travel
   D. where the cylinder is coolest

   1.____

2. After boring or honing a worn gasoline engine cylinder, it is good practice to clean the grit out of the pores of the cast iron block.
   In the absence of continuous cleaning facilities, this is done BEST by cleaning the cylinder with
   A. gasoline
   B. hot water and soap
   C. benzene
   D. kerosene and waste

   2.____

3. One of the BEST ways to check the concentricity of the valve guide and valve seat is by the use of a(n)
   A. expanding reamer
   B. dial indicator
   C. inside micrometer
   D. bevel protractor

   3.____

4. The thimble of a micrometer is slightly before the .475" graduation on the barrel.
   If the thimble reading is between .018" and .019", and the reading on the Vernier is .006", then the full opening is
   A. .4946"   B. .4696"   C. .4686"   D. .4936"

   4.____

5. The sum of 9/16", 11/32", 15/64", and 1 3/32" is MOST NEARLY
   A. 2.234"   B. 2.134"   C. 2.334"   D. 2.214"

   5.____

6. The diameter of a circle whose circumference is 14.5" is MOST NEARLY
   A. 4.62"   B. 4.81"   C. 4.72"   D. 4.51"

   6.____

7. A *literate* worker is one who is MOST NEARLY
   A. unlearned   B. sinuous   C. educated   D. impervious

   7.____

8. If a mechanic is told that a certain repair job is *feasible*, this means it is MOST NEARLY
   A. laborious   B. moderate   C. practicable   D. easy

   8.____

9. A mechanic who is *dexterous* at his job is one who is MOST NEARLY
   A. proficient   B. devious   C. devoted   D. impartial

   9.____

10. To obtain a certain type of fit, an intentional difference in the dimensions of the mating parts is usually specified on the blueprints.
    This intentional difference is called
    A. allowance   B. tolerance   C. clearance   D. nominal

11. A micro-inch is
    A. an inch measured on a micrometer
    B. an inch measured with a microscope
    C. a ten-thousandth of an inch
    D. one-millionth of an inch

12. Assuming the bore of a gasoline engine cylinder measures 3 inches and the piston for this cylinder has a stroke of 4 inches, the piston displacement, in cubic inches per stroke of piston, will be MOST NEARLY
    A. 36   B. 48   C. 32   D. 28

13. If an engine cylinder should be worn in such a way that there is a taper of 0.008" from top to bottom, the piston ring and gap, when traveling up and down over this surface, will be opening and closing MOST NEARLY
    A. 0.008"   B. 0.016"   C. 0.020"   D. 0.024"

14. In freezing weather, a lead-acid storage battery should NOT have a specific gravity reading
    A. above 1.250   B. above 1.235
    C. below 1.250   D. of 1.285

15. In servicing a worn and badly tapered gasoline engine cylinder that has quite a *step* at the bottom of the ring travel, it is BEST to
    A. start the honing in the unworn area below the ring travel
    B. start the honing in the center of the ring travel
    C. start the honing in the unworn area above the ring travel
    D. just fit an oversized piston for the top part of the cylinder

16. In a gasoline engine, if the distributor breaker points are replaced twice as often as the generator brushes, but the generator brushes are replaced one-quarter as often as the spark plugs, then it is CORRECT to say that the spark plugs are replaced _____ as often as the distributor breaker points.
    A. twice   B. four times   C. one-half   D. one-quarter

17. In the four stroke cycle gasoline engine, the sequence of the steps in each cylinder to complete a cycle is which one of the following?
    A. power stroke, compression stroke, exhaust stroke
    B. compression stroke, exhaust stroke, power stroke
    C. exhaust stroke, compression stroke, power stroke
    D. compression stroke, power stroke, exhaust stroke

18. The cutting edge of a cold chisel should be tempered at a temperature corresponding to a color of
    A. blue   B. pale blue   C. light straw   D. purple

19. To properly service a clutch, the type that is commonly used on gasoline engines, it is important that the face or frictional surface of the flywheel should run true blue within a tolerance of MOST NEARLY
    A. .006" B. .012" C. .018" D. .025"

20. The BEST way to check a warped cylinder head is by means of a
    A. straight edge
    B. surface gauge
    C. feeler gauge
    D. dial indicator

21. Upon inspecting a cam ground piston skirt, while cold, it will be found that the skirt is USUALLY
    A. circular in cross-section
    B. smaller in diameter than the piston head
    C. widest at wrist pin bosses
    D. oval in cross-section

22. If a transmission main drive gear, having 20 teeth, rotates at 450 RPM. and drives a countershaft drive gear at 300 RPM, the TOTAL number of teeth on the countershaft drive gear will be
    A. 30 B. 15 C. 25 D. 45

23. In reference to the piston, wrist pin, and connecting rod assembly of a gasoline engine, it is NOT common practice to ever
    A. fix the pin to the piston by a set screw
    B. allow the pin to rotate in both the connecting rod and piston bosses
    C. anchor the pin to connecting rod
    D. use precision type split bearings at the wrist pin end of connecting rod

24. Upon dismantling a gasoline engine, it was found that the piston rings were stuck in the grooves, not being free to rotate.
    This was MOST LIKELY caused by
    A. operating the engine with spark setting in advanced position
    B. the thermostat maintaining too low an engine temperature
    C. dirty or contaminated lubricating oil
    D. using the wrong type of spark plugs in the engine

25. Many gasoline engines today are being built with cylinder heads of cast aluminum alloy.
    The reason for using aluminum is MAINLY because it
    A. is a better conductor of heat
    B. will not rust
    C. has less expansion per degree F. than cast iron
    D. is lighter in weight

26. A gasoline engine that utilizes a rocker arm for operating intake and exhaust valves is COMMONLY classified as a(n) _____ engine.
    A. T-head B. I-head C. L-head D. 2 cam haft

27. Assuming that a sliding gear transmission is so built that there is a gear ratio between the transmission main drive gear and the countershaft drive gear of 1.5 to 1, and, with gears shifted to low speed, there is an additional gear ratio between the countershaft low-speed gear and the low-and-reverse mainshaft gear of 1.5 to 1, then, for the propeller shaft to rotate 200 RPM, the crankshaft will have to rotate MOST NEARLY _____ RPM.
    A. 450   B. 600   C. 500   D. 300

28. Which one of the following statements concerning shop safety precautions would you select as being CORRECT?
    A. Starting a machine while it is being adjusted or repaired is a good practice.
    B. Guards may be removed by the operator to expedite the work.
    C. Gears, pulleys, and belts should be guarded to a height of 6 feet above the floor.
    D. Knowledge and care will not prevent most accidents.

29. The breaker point on a six lobe cam distributor are USUALLY brought and held together by means of a
    A. cam   B. spring   C. worm gear   D. timer

30. Pitted or burned distributor breaker points may BEST be refaced by using
    A. emery cloth   B. sandpaper
    C. an oil stone   D. a steel file

31. The piece of equipment commonly used on many gasoline engines that is composed of such parts as yokes, struts, release levers, pressure springs, and pilot bearing is MOST LIKELY a
    A. clutch   B. transmission
    C. torque converter   D. differential

32. Upon installing a reconditioned clutch in a gasoline engine that uses a clutch foot pedal, the proper adjustment to make on the clutch pedal *free play* on most cars is MOST NEARLY
    A. 2"   B. 1"   C. 0.25"   D. none

33. A gasoline engine cylinder that is worn and has been found to have a taper of .012" can BEST be reconditioned before being placed into operation again by
    A. replacing the oil ring backed with an expander
    B. replacing the original oil ring with a very active one
    C. reboring or honing the cylinder and using an oversized piston
    D. reboring or honing the cylinder and using an undersized piston

34. In the S.A.E. Standard Series of Screw Threads, a screw size 7/16"-20 would be classified as
    A. NC   B. NF   C. EF   D. NS

35. In the 90° V-type eight cylinder gasoline engine, the number of *throws* or *cranks* the crankshaft is USUALLY
    A. eight B. six C. four D. two

36. Grinding and refinishing exhaust valves and seats on most gasoline engines should be done so that the seat angle (relative to the centerline passing through the valve guide is USUALLY
    A. 60° B. 25° C. 35° D. 45°

37. An automotive gasoline engine is being completely reconditioned, including the fitting of the valve stem in its guide.
    In the absence of specific information from the manufacturer, the proper exhaust valve stem to guide clearance for MOST engines should be
    A. .003" B. .010" C. .018" D. .030"

38. An instrument which can be used generally to measure inside and outside measurements without making any calculations to called a _____ caliper.
    A. Gear tooth
    B. Vernier
    C. Telescoping
    D. Micrometer

Questions 39-40.

DIRECTIONS: Questions 39 and 40 are based upon the following paragraph. Use only the information contained in this paragraph in answering these questions.

With the engine running at normal idling speed, and the engine hood open, attach the vacuum gauge to the intake manifold. The vacuum gauge should read about 18 to 21 inches, and the pointer should be steady. A needle fluctuating between 10 and 15 inches may indicate a defective cylinder-head, gasket, or valve. An extremely low reading indicates a leak in the intake manifold or gaskets. Accelerate the engine with full throttle momentarily. Notice if the gauge indicator fails to drop to approximately 2 inches as the throttle is opened, and recoil to at least 24 inches as the throttle is closed. If so, this may be an indication of diluted oil, poor piston ring sealing, or an abnormal restriction in the exhaust, carburetor, or air cleaner. The above readings apply to sea level. There will be approximately 1 inch drop for each 1,000 feet of altitude.

39. If a vacuum test is made on a properly operating engine at an altitude of 3,000 feet, the vacuum gauge should read MOST NEARLY
    A. 12" B. 15" C. 13" D. 24"

40. If a vacuum test is made on an engine which has an abnormal restriction in the exhaust, this will be evidenced by
    A. a leak in the intake manifold
    B. the gauge indicator failing to drop to approximately 3 inches on opening the throttle
    C. the gauge fluctuating around 12 inches
    D. a steady high gauge reading

41. The PROPER thing to do in checking the fuel pump of a gasoline engine which will NOT start because of insufficient gas is to
    A. remove the pump from the engine in order to check
    B. disconnect the fuel line from the tank to the pump and run the pump
    C. disconnect the pump to the carburetor line and run the pump
    D. make sure that the external plugs over the pump valve are loosened before running the pump

42. It is a good policy to occasionally change the brake fluid in a hydraulic brake system.
    However, before refilling with fresh brake fluid, it is advisable to flush out the system with
    A. alcohol   B. kerosene   C. gasoline   D. a light oil

43. Battery hydrometers are calibrated to give the correct specific gravity readings of lead-acid storage batteries at a temperature of
    A. 70°F.   B. 80°F.   C. 32°F.   D. 60°F.

44. In a gasoline engine, if grease should leak into the cooling system by way of the water pump and, in addition, combustion gases should leak into the coolant, a test of the coolant will be found MOST LIKELY to be
    A. slightly alkaline   B. slightly acid
    C. strongly alkaline   D. free of foreign deposits

45. Reverse flushing of a clogged gasoline engine block and radiator cooling system is done PROPERLY by
    A. not removing the thermostat out of the engine block
    B. connecting the flushing gun at the bottom of the engine block
    C. using air and water
    D. using low pressure steam

46. In an automotive gasoline engine water cooling system, the water distributing tube is USUALLY found
    A. at the top of the radiator   B. at the bottom of the radiator
    C. on top of the cylinder head   D. in the engine block

47. When reference is made to the *compression ratio* of an automotive gasoline engine, this is BEST described to be the
    A. volume above the piston at top dead center
    B. displacement volume as the piston moves down to bottom dead center
    C. total volume of a cylinder divided by its clearance volume
    D. displacement volume of a cylinder divided by its clearance volume

48. When the piston of a gasoline engine is said to be in *rock* position, it is meant that the
    A. piston has reached rock bottom of its stroke
    B. crankshaft cannot move without causing the piston to move

C. crankshaft can move about 20° without causing the valves to open or close
D. crankshaft can move about 15° without causing the piston to move up or down

49. Regarding the automatic transmission which today is very popular with most automobile engines, the features that are found on MOST of the various transmission units are 49.____
    A. hydraulic controls
    B. full power automatic shifting planetaries
    C. double pinion planetary full torque shifts
    D. split torque fluid drives

50. An air leak between the intake manifold and the engine block can BEST be checked by 50.____
    A. applying a soapy solution to each joint on the block
    B. applying a little gasoline at each manifold and block joint
    C. using a heavy oil at each joint in the block
    D. listening for the sucking sound of air entering the joint

KEY (CORRECT ANSWERS)

1.	A	11.	D	21.	D	31.	A	41.	C
2.	B	12.	D	22.	A	32.	B	42.	A
3.	B	13.	D	23.	D	33.	C	43.	B
4.	C	14.	C	24.	C	34.	B	44.	B
5.	A	15.	A	25.	A	35.	C	45.	C
6.	A	16.	A	26.	B	36.	D	46.	D
7.	C	17.	D	27.	A	37.	A	47.	C
8.	C	18.	C	28.	C	38.	B	48.	D
9.	A	19.	A	29.	B	39.	B	49.	A
10.	A	20.	A	30.	C	40.	B	50.	B

TEST 2

DIRECTIONS: Each question or incomplete statement is followed by several suggested answers or completions. Select the one that BEST answers the question or completes the statement. *PRINT THE LETTER OF THE CORRECT ANSWER IN THE SPACE AT THE RIGHT.*

1. The LEAST likely reason for a shunt generator to lose most of its residual magnetism is due to
   A. alternating current fed to the field winding
   B. too much vibration of generator
   C. excessive operating temperature
   D. the generator delivering too much current

   1.____

2. In today's modern high compression engines, hard starting, rough running, and poor gas economy are LEAST likely to be due to the electrical system having
   A. high resistor plugs   B. cracked distributor cap
   C. worn insulation   D. fouled plugs

   2.____

3. The method that is NOT used for detecting cracks that may exist in a gasoline engine block or head is by
   A. dye penetrants   B. pressure testing
   C. the sheradizing method   D. the magnetic method

   3.____

4. Before making any front wheel alignment checks on a car, such as toe-in and camber, it is ADVISABLE to
   A. first make sure that the vehicle has no load in it
   B. jack up the front wheels so that they are free to turn
   C. inflate the tire to recommended pressure
   D. first check the wheel brakes

   4.____

5. When replacing a new cylinder head gasket on a gasoline engine, it is good practice to tighten the cylinder head nuts with a torque wrench to a gauge reading, in foot pounds, of MOST NEARLY
   a. 60   B. 40   C. 90   D. 25

   5.____

6. Assume that a carburetor has been reconditioned and the mechanic replaced the metering rod with one of a larger diameter than the original one.
   On operating the carburetor, it is MOST LIKELY that
   A. at idling, the engine would run at a higher speed
   B. the engine will receive a leaner mixture
   C. the carburetor would easily flood
   D. there will be very little noticeable difference in engine operation

   6.____

7. A mechanic, running a test on a gasoline engine, has noted on the job sheet that the cam angle is 32 degrees.
   From this information, it is evident that the mechanic is running a test on the
   A. camshaft   B. ignition system
   C. front wheel   D. valve timing

   7.____

2 (#2)

8. An idler gear that is often found in a sliding gear transmission is used MAINLY
   A. when more power is desired
   B. when engine is idling and car is not in motion
   C. to reverse the direction of rotation
   D. to obtain a reduced gear speed

8.____

9. Assume that a compression test is made of a six-cylinder gasoline engine having a compression ratio of 6.5 to 1. A reading of 95 lbs. was obtained for cylinders #1, #2, #4, and #6, 52 lbs. for cylinder #3, and 71 lbs. for cylinder #5. Upon squirting engine oil into the cylinder and rechecking pressures again, it was found that cylinder #5 read 93 lbs., and cylinder #3 read 52 lbs.
   From the above results, it is MOST probable that the
   A. exhaust valve on cylinder #5 does not seat properly
   B. cylinder #5 piston rings or cylinder are worn
   C. cylinder #5 piston rings are worn
   D. oil leaks past the cylinder #5 valve guides

9.____

10. In operating a gasoline engine using a manual gear shift, if it becomes difficult to shift, especially into low gear, the trouble is MOST LIKELY due to the
    A. clutch plate not burning
    B. clutch shaft spines tapering toward the end
    C. clutch facing being too dry
    D. clearance between the pressure plate and the flywheel being too great

10.____

11. In reference to the internal combustion engine, the term *mechanical efficiency* is frequently used.
    The meaning of this term is BEST defined as the
    A. thermal efficiency divided by the volumetric efficiency
    B. thermal efficiency multiplied by the volumetric efficiency
    C. indicated horsepower divided by the brake horsepower
    D. brake horsepower divided by the indicated horsepower

11.____

12. In calculating the *indicated* horsepower of a gasoline engine by means of a formula, the item that is NOT considered in the calculations is USUALLY the
    A. number of power strokes per cycle
    B. pressure exerted on the piston during the power stroke
    C. diameter of the piston
    D. length of the piston

12.____

13. The type of gear drive that will operate MORE quietly under similar conditions in a differential unit is one consisting of a _____ gear.
    A. worm and
    B. drive pinion and spur bevel
    C. drive pinion and hypoid
    D. drive pinion and spiral-bevel

13.____

14. The differential of many trucks is very often made up of a worm and gear drive. In reference to this type of drive, which one of the following statements is TRUE?
    A. The worm is usually made of bronze and the worm gear of steel
    B. The rear worm bearing need not be very rugged since it takes very little thrust.

14.____

C. This type of drive allows a large speed reduction.
D. This type of drive is not recommended because the worm must be mounted on top of the worm gear.

15. It is common practice today for some manufacturers to make the outside surface of aluminum alloy pistons highly resistant to wear by
    A. spheroidizing   B. case hardening
    C. anodizing   D. annealing

16. The ease with which the front wheels of a car return to the straight-ahead position after having completed a turn is due to the
    A. toe-in   B. side thrust   C. camber   D. caster

17. If you should be driving a truck downhill on a slippery road and the rear end of the truck begins to skid to the right, it would be BEST for you to
    A. apply the brakes slowly and disengage the clutch
    B. let up on the gas pedal slowly and turn the wheels to the right
    C. turn the wheels to the right and disengage the clutch
    D. apply the brakes hard and turn the wheels to the left

18. If a *no load test* is made on the electric starting motor used on most passenger cars today, it will be found that the number of amperes the motor would draw, at its rated speed, is MOST NEARLY
    A. 70   B. 105   C. 210   D. 20

19. By the correct valve timing of a gasoline engine is meant the proper opening and closing of valves with reference to the
    A. carburetor mixing jets   B. distributor setting
    C. position of piston   D. cylinder compression ratio

20. The *primary* ignition circuit of an automotive gasoline engine is composed of the battery,
    A. starting motor, generator, ignition coil, spark plugs
    B. ammeter, ignition coil, ignition switch, distributor rotor
    C. ammeter, ignition switch, ignition coil, secondary winding
    D. ammeter, ignition switch, coil primary winding, breaker points

21. To increase the ampere-hour capacity of a lead-acid storage battery, it is necessary to increase the
    A. number of cells   B. amount of the electrolyte
    C. number of plates per cell   D. voltage of the cells

22. Intake and exhaust manifolds, used on the present day gasoline engine, are designed and built so that their walls come in contact with each other in order to
    A. prevent condensation of fuel vapor
    B. save space
    C. get better valve action
    D. reduce vaporization

23. By referring to the *torque* of a gasoline engine crankshaft is meant the
    A. ratio of crankshaft to rear axle
    B. horsepower developed at axles
    C. turning moment of the crankshaft
    D. permissible bend of flexibility in the crankshaft

24. Upon making a running test of the braking system of a car, it was found that the brake drum on one of the wheels ran abnormally cool.
    From this result, the auto mechanic will find that this is MOST LIKELY due to
    A. worn brake lining
    B. a broken return spring
    C. the brake drum surface worn too smooth
    D. an inoperative brake

25. The factor that has no relation upon the determination of proper wheel alignment is
    A. pivot inclination   B. toe-out
    C. caster   D. drop-center rim

26. If a gasoline engine is continued in operation with the contact points of a reverse current relay or *cut-out* being fused together, the result would MOST LIKELY be to
    A. *run down* the battery
    B. reverse the current through the voltage coils
    C. demagnetize the relay iron core
    D. overcharge the battery

27. Starting motors that mesh directly with the flywheel gears and are used on most modern cars today are designed to give an engine cranking speed, in RMP, of MOST NEARLY
    A. 150   B. 250   C. 350   D. 400

28. The type of electric starting motor used on most cars today, because of its high starting torque, is USUALLY the _____ type.
    A. shunt wound   B. series wound
    C. compound wound   D. capacitor

29. If an engine, while running, has a noticeable piston slap, it is LIKELY that this is caused by
    A. worn cylinder walls
    B. excessively advanced ignition timing
    C. worn main bearings
    D. worn end-thrust bearings

30. Vapor-lock in a gasoline engine is MOST LIKELY due to
    A. an over-rich gas-air mixture
    B. fuel forming bubbles in the gas line
    C. a tear in the fuel pump diaphragm
    D. the carburetor being clogged with dirt

31. In starting on a cold day, the choke is pulled out.
    The PRIMARY reason for this is that it
    A. allows more fuel to enter the carburetor enriching the mixture
    B. increases the amount of air in the carburetor
    C. reduces the amount of fuel entering the carburetor
    D. speeds up the supply of air and fuel to the motor

31.____

32. When driving at night toward another car, the CORRECT procedure as to lights is to put on
    A. your high beams
    B. your low beams
    C. whatever lights the other driver uses
    D. your parking lights

32.____

33. The liquid in a battery in good condition is
    A. an acid solution   B. a caustic solution
    C. a salt water solution   D. water only

33.____

34. The ammeter of an automobile indicates the flow of electric current
    A. from the battery to the starting motor
    B. outside of the starting circuit
    C. to the lights
    D. to and from the storage battery

34.____

35. Manifolds are used to conduct
    A. gases out of an engine only   B. gases into an engine only
    C. gases into or out of an engine   D. heat into the piston

35.____

36. Of the following, the one NOT concerned with transmitting the driving power from the engine to the driving wheels is the
    A. clutch   B. drive shaft   C. flywheel   D. front axle

36.____

37. To prevent short circuits in the electrical system of a car, we use
    A. a layer of rust   B. insulation   C. oil   D. water

37.____

38. An alert auto mechanic knows that if the center tread of the tires of a car show little wear while the outer edges show considerable wear, it is a sign of driving
    A. on over-inflated tires   B. on properly inflated tires
    C. on under-inflated tires   D. too fast for proper braking

38.____

39. The working parts of an engine are lubricated by
    A. grease in the transmission   B. oil in the transmission
    C. oil from the carburetor   D. oil in the crankcase

39.____

40. The water in the cooling system of a car should be
    A. acid   B. alkaline   C. neutral   D. salty

40.____

41. Of the following, the type of service that a mechanic should be personally concerned with is
    A. adjustment of small parts such as spark plugs
    B. daily inspection of vehicles for gas, oil, and water
    C. general overhauls of large unit assemblies
    D. replacement of unit assemblies such as fuel pumps

42. The part of a car which allows one wheel to go faster than the other in going around a corner is the
    A. brake
    B. differential
    C. slip joint
    D. universal joint

43. If the temperature gauge indicates the engine is getting overheated,
    A. allow it to cool down
    B. pour cold water in immediately
    C. pour hot water in immediately
    D. pour in a cooling antifreeze at one

44. The clutch pedal is being used properly when you
    A. press it down in order to change gears
    B. push it down to the floor going down hill
    C. rest your left foot on it
    D. use it only for emergencies

45. The part of an engine in which the gasoline and air burns is the
    A. camshaft   B. carburetor   C. cylinder   D. piston

46. The part of an engine which mixes the gasoline with the air is the
    A. camshaft   B. carburetor   C. cylinder   D. piston

47. The function of a generator in a car is to supply the
    A. ignition system with current
    B. lights with current
    C. battery with current to recharge it
    D. starting motor with current

48. The accelerator pedal is used for controlling the
    A. carburetor throttle
    B. ignition system
    C. oil pressure
    D. spark plug

49. Alcohol is put into the radiator of an automobile in cold weather because it _____ the _____ point of the mixture.
    A. lowers; boiling
    B. lowers; freezing
    C. raises; boiling
    D. raises; freezing

50. A good rule to follow when driving in winter when roads may be icy is to 50._____
    A. be prepared to come to a quick stop when the car starts to skid
    B. be sure of your brakes so you can come down hard on them
    C. keep your speed down and turn the wheels in the direction of any skid that may occur
    D. put the car in neutral and gently pat the brakes into position

KEY (CORRECT ANSWERS)

1. D	11. D	21. C	31. A	41. B
2. A	12. D	22. A	32. B	42. B
3. C	13. C	23. C	33. A	43. A
4. C	14. C	24. D	34. D	44. A
5. A	15. C	25. D	35. C	45. C
6. B	16. D	26. D	36. D	46. B
7. B	17. B	27. A	37. B	47. C
8. C	18. A	28. B	38. C	48. A
9. C	19. C	29. A	39. D	49. B
10. B	20. D	30. B	40. C	50. C

TEST 3

DIRECTIONS: Each question or incomplete statement is followed by several suggested answers or completions. Select the one that BEST answers the question or completes the statement. *PRINT THE LETTER OF THE CORRECT ANSWER IN THE SPACE AT THE RIGHT.*

1. A sudden falling back of about 5 points on a vacuum gauge with the engine running under 15 m.p.h. indicates
    A. a leaky manifold gasket
    B. loose or worn valve guides
    C. points are pitted
    D. a burned valve in one cylinder

    1.____

2. When the vacuum gauge needle drifts regularly between 5 and 19, it means that
    A. the carburetor is poorly adjusted
    B. there is a compression leak between cylinders
    C. the exhaust system is clogged
    D. the ignition advance is incorrect

    2.____

3. A bent steering arm will affect
    A. caster
    B. toe-out
    C. camber
    D. king pin inclination

    3.____

4. When the accelerator is depressed quickly, the
    A. vacuum in the intake manifold increases
    B. vacuum in the intake manifold remains the same
    C. pressure in the float chamber increases
    D. pressure in the intake manifold increases

    4.____

5. When an air cleaner has collected an excessive amount of road dust, the
    A. mixture becomes leaner
    B. compression pressure is increased
    C. volumetric efficiency increases
    D. mixture becomes richer

    5.____

6. The full weight of the rear of a vehicle is carried by the axle shaft of a
    A. semi-floating axle
    B. full floating axle
    C. three-quarter floating axle
    D. jack shaft

    6.____

7. Certain engines are designed with the spark plug port over the exhaust valve because
    A. this keeps spark plugs at proper temperature
    B. this design reduces detonation
    C. spark plugs last longer
    D. this prevents loss of power

    7.____

8. The MAIN advantage of valve seat inserts is to
    A. reduce wear on the valve face
    B. reduce frequency of valve grinding
    C. keep clearance on valve more nearly constant
    D. increase the life of the valves

    8.____

9. The harmonic balancer on a crankshaft is used
   A. as a flywheel
   B. to neutralize torsional crankshaft vibration
   C. to offset the weight of the flywheel
   D. to offset the weight of the connecting rods

10. Sealed clutch release bearings require
    A. cup grease
    B. spicer grease
    C. engine oil
    D. no grease

11. The pressure which forces the gas from the fuel pump to the carburetor is produced by
    A. the expanding action of the diaphragm spring
    B. the upstroke of the pump arm
    C. the vacuum created in the pump
    D. decreased pressure in the fuel bowl

12. A low reading on the oil gauge is a PROBABLE indication of
    A. high engine temperature
    B. bearings too tight
    C. oil dilution
    D. too heavy a grade of oil

13. Pressure plate springs are checked for
    A. number of coils
    B. thickness of coils
    C. weight
    D. height and pressure

14. Of the following, the CHIEF advantage of *over-drive* in modern transmissions is that it
    A. allows the engine to run slower at high car speeds
    B. allows the car to coast on hills
    C. requires less shifting
    D. provides greater power at high speeds

15. The oil circuit through a gear type oil pump is
    A. between the gear teeth
    B. over the gear teeth
    C. under the gear teeth
    D. between the gear teeth and pump housing

16. Good compression in an engine depends upon
    A. ignition timing
    B. carburetor adjustment
    C. type of gasoline used
    D. condition of rings and valves

17. The differential pinion gear meshes with the ring gear below the horizontal center line of the ring gear on a _____ gear.
    A. spiral bevel
    B. hypoid
    C. spur
    D. straight bevel

18. Heavy flank contact on teeth between drive pinion gear and ring gear will result in
    A. excessive play between gear teeth
    B. noisy gear operation
    C. broken drive pinion bearings
    D. excessive end play in differential case bearings

19. Back firing in the carburetor is caused by
    A. too rich a mixture
    B. excess oil in combustion chamber
    C. faulty fuel pump
    D. too lean a mixture

20. A worn metering pin will cause
    A. fast idle speed
    B. rich mixture under load
    C. leaner mixture under load
    D. engine stalling

21. Broken gear teeth on differential side gears will cause a
    A. squeak when the car is traveling in a straight ahead direction
    B. broken axle
    C. knock in rear end when car is making a turn
    D. loss of power

22. Excessive accumulation of soft carbon deposit on intake valve stems and under intake valve head is an indication that the
    A. intake valve guides are worn
    B. carburetor is set too rich
    C. gasoline is stale
    D. spark is weak, causing poor compression

23. The MOST popular type of clutch used today in modern vehicle is the _____ clutch.
    A. wet
    B. 3-plate
    C. multiple-disc
    D. single plate

24. When a Timken bearing is used in a transmission, it is readily identified by
    A. its tapered rollers
    B. the concave races
    C. the barrel-shaped rollers
    D. an exclusive retainer design

25. The MOST common type of cooling system in use today is
    A. pump or pressure
    B. splash and gravity
    C. radiator and fan
    D. thermosyphon

26. Scoring of pistons and cylinder walls is caused by
    A. pistons fitting too loose
    B. infrequent oil changes
    C. high piston temperatures
    D. insufficient piston clearances

27. Regardless of the number of cylinders, the distributor of the magneto MUST always be driven at _____ speed.
    A. engine
    B. one-half engine
    C. twice engine
    D. constant

28. The capacity of a battery is determined by the
    A. rate at which a battery can be charged
    B. quantity of electrolyte the case can hold
    C. rate at which it can be discharged
    D. voltage of the battery

29. While driving along the road, all lights suddenly flare up and burn out because
    A. a fuse blew out
    B. a short circuit occurred in a lighting wire
    C. a wire became loose on the ground switch
    D. the battery cable broke off

30. A solenoid is often used to operate the
    A. generator   B. starter   C. battery   D. ignition

31. In a storage battery, the H_2SO_4 after reacting with the active material in the plates forms H_2O^4 in the electrolyte when
    A. a battery is discharging   B. it is being charged
    C. it is gassing   D. it is sulphated

32. Voltage and current regulators prevent
    A. overload of starter   B. static in radio
    C. spark plug failure   D. overcharging of battery

33. Batteries not in service will become discharged because of
    A. drop in specific gravity   B. open circuit
    C. lack of agitation   D. local action

34. Throwing of solder from generator commutator is caused USUALLY by
    A. poor insulation   B. overload
    C. underload   D. high tension current

35. A low generator output with a fully charged battery indicates
    A. worn or pitted vibrator points
    B. eroded battery terminals
    C. correct generator control
    D. the vibrator armature spring is too weak

36. Generator output control or regulation is based on controlling the
    A. armature magnetism   B. field current
    C. third brush   D. polarity

37. When an armature is revolved between the pole pieces of a growler, a heavy vibration is caused by a _____ voltage current induced in a(n) _____ coil.
    A. low; open   B. high; open
    C. high; short-circuited   D. low; short-circuited

38. In shunt wound generators, full control of the generator output is obtained through the use of
    A. third brush
    B. current regulator
    C. voltage regulator
    D. current and voltage regulator

39. The function of the cut-out relay in the battery generator circuit is to
    A. regulate the generator voltage
    B. regulate the generator amperage
    C. prevent the loss of battery current
    D. prevent the battery from being overcharged

40. A cracked distributor cap usually would cause misfiring because of
    A. poor contact
    B. short circuit
    C. high resistance
    D. overloading

41. In a sealed beam headlight, the
    A. lamp is sealed in the car fender
    B. light rays are sealed within the lamp
    C. lens and reflector are sealed together
    D. light beam is sealed in one direction on the road

42. The capacity of a storage battery is determined by the
    A. number of cells
    B. composition of the case
    C. number of plates
    D. shape of the battery

43. Armature *neutral point* is obtained by
    A. adjusting position of brushes
    B. neutralizing residual magnetism
    C. aligning the ignition contacts
    D. unmeshing the starter pinion gear

44. Cam angle is increased by
    A. increasing the point gap
    B. decreasing the point gap
    C. centrifugal advance
    D. greater advance

45. A shorted armature coil
    A. must be shellacked
    B. may be corrected by undercutting the commutator
    C. must have commutator refaced
    D. must be baked

46. A steady miss at all speeds is USUALLY caused by
    A. clogged low speed jet
    B. low float level
    C. defective spark plug
    D. poor condenser

47. When testing an armature, if the sawblade vibrates, it indicates that the armature is
    A. grounded
    B. correct
    C. short-circuited
    D. open-circuited

48. If an electric gasoline gauge registers full at all times, trouble is in the
    A. wire to the tank
    B. line to the switch
    C. gasoline line
    D. battery terminal

49. The Dyer Starter Drive
    A. is an over-running clutch drive
    B. works like the Bendix Drive
    C. rotates the starter pinion while it is moved towards the flywheel
    D. has a special gear reduction

50. The MOST accurate method used to time the ignition of an engine is by
    A. locating the piston position with a wire
    B. use of neon timing light
    C. watching for contact point opening
    D. watching valve position

KEY (CORRECT ANSWERS)

1.	D	11.	A	21.	C	31.	A	41.	C
2.	B	12.	C	22.	A	32.	D	42.	C
3.	B	13.	D	23.	D	33.	D	43.	A
4.	D	14.	A	24.	A	34.	B	44.	B
5.	D	15.	D	25.	A	35.	C	45.	B
6.	A	16.	D	26.	D	36.	B	46.	C
7.	B	17.	B	27.	B	37.	C	47.	C
8.	B	18.	B	28.	C	38.	D	48.	A
9.	B	19.	D	29.	D	39.	C	49.	C
10.	D	20.	B	30.	B	40.	B	50.	B

EXAMINATION SECTION
TEST 1

DIRECTIONS: Each question or incomplete statement is followed by several suggested answers or completions. Select the one that BEST answers the question or completes the statement. *PRINT THE LETTER OF THE CORRECT ANSWER IN THE SPACE AT THE RIGHT.*

1. Of the following, the ACCEPTED method reconditioning a connected rod big end bore is to
    A. use a press to return the rod cap's diameter to standard size
    B. hone the bore to the next standard bearing oversize
    C. remove an amount of stock equal to the oversize from the split on the cap and then hone to standard size
    D. remove equal amounts of stock from both the cap and the rod at the split and then hone to standard size

    1.____

2. After a cylinder that has a 3,000 inch bore has been honed, it is found to be tapered .003 inch. The removed aluminum piston is to be reused.
    The piston should be
    A. cleaned and reinstalled
    B. knurled to increase the diameter of the entire skirt by .003 inch
    C. knurled at the top of the skirt to 3.001 inches and at the bottom of the skirt to 3.000 inches
    D. knurled at the top of the skirt to 3.000 inches and at the bottom of the skirt to 3.001 inches

    2.____

3. Of the following, the PROPER sequence of operations in reconditioning valve seats for replacement valves that have oversize stems is to
    A. clean guide, ream guide, grind seat, and narrow seat
    B. clean guide, grind seat, ream guide, and narrow seat
    C. clean guide, narrow seat, grind seat, and ream guide
    D. grind seat, narrow seat, clean guide, and ream guide

    3.____

4. An engine cylinder measures 3.520 inches at the bottom of the bore and 3.529 inches near the top. The factory bore measured .500 inches.
    New pistons to be installed after boring should GENERALLY be _____ inch oversize.
    A. .010   B. .020   C. .030   D. .050

    4.____

5. An engine vacuum gauge used to measure intake-manifold pressure reads in
    A. pounds per square inch   B. inches of mercury
    C. pounds per square foot   D. ounces per inch

    5.____

55

6. A hydrometer is being used to determine the specific gravity of a lead-acid storage battery which is at a temperature of 120 degrees Fahrenheit. The hydrometer gives a reading of 1.230.
   The true specific gravity of the electrolyte at that temperature is MOST NEARLY
   A. 1.198   B. 1.205   C. 1.230   D. 1,246

7. The micrometer reading shown in the figure at the right is
   A. .525"
   B. .555"
   C. .562"
   D. .568"

8. In connection with the inspection and the turning or the grinding of brake drums on passenger cars, the BEST practice is to
   A. weld a cracked brake drum
   B. turn or grind the brake drum if it is out of round by more than .060 inches
   C. turn or grind the drums in pairs so that both front drums are the same diameter and both back drums are the same diameter
   D. increase the standard drum diameter to a maximum of 0.12 inches by turning or grinding

9. Of the following, the BEST tool to use to undercut mica on the commutator of a starting motor is a
   A. round nose chisel   B. hacksaw blade
   C. flat chisel   D. hand reamer

10. In a properly adjusted gasoline-powered automotive engine, the MAXIMUM percentage of the energy in the gasoline that can be transferred by the engine to the driving wheels of an automobile is MOST NEARLY
    A. 20%   B. 40%   C. 60%   D 80%

11. The lever length of a torque wrench is 24 inches.
    If a force of 50 pounds is properly applied at the handle when torquing a nut, the applied torque, in foot-pounds, is
    A. 50   B. 100   C. 400   D. 1200

12. While a fuel pump discharge pressure test is being performed, it is found that the pressure drops rapidly when the engine is stopped.
    This indicates a
    A. leaking pump-outlet valve   B. leaking suction hose
    C. leaking pump-diaphragm   D. normal condition

13. Of the following, the size of copper conductor which has the GREATEST current-carrying capacity is _____ AWG.
    A. 12   B. 8   C. 0   D. 000

14. Of the following, the statement pertaining to soldering which is MOST correct is:
    A. 60/40 solder would best be used for automotive-body repair
    B. Acid flux should not be used on copper parts such as radiators
    C. Main flux should be used on electrical connections
    D. The strength of the joint is not dependent on the joint thickness

15. When a car axle ring gear and pinion is being adjusted, the ring gear is moved toward the pinion
    This movement will change the tooth contact toward the _____ of the ring gear.
    A. toe   B. heel   C. dedendum   D. addendum

16. An automotive hydraulic brake system has a 1 inch diameter master cylinder and a 1.2 inch diameter wheel cylinder.
    The force applied by the wheel cylinder piston will be MOST NEARL _____ the force applied to the master cylinder piston.
    A. equal to   B. 1.44 times   C. 1.20 times   D. 0.833 times

17. Of the following, the statement regarding the rebuilding of hydraulic brake master cylinder which is MOST correct is that
    A. a light coat of grease should be applied to the parts during assembly to prevent rusting
    B. very light scratches in the bore can be polished out with emery cloth
    C. the parts must be cleaned in denatured alcohol
    D. deep scratches and pitting can be removed by honing to permit cylinder reuse

18. An automobile is standing still with the engine running and the clutch disengaged.
    Of the following, the part of the clutch assembly that is stationary is the
    A. flywheel   B. clutch cover
    C. pressure plate   D. clutch disk

19. Of the following liquids, the BEST one to use for cleaning automotive cylinders after they have been honed is
    A. hot, soapy water   B. gasoline
    C. turpentine   D. kerosene

20. In an in-line gasoline-powered automotive engine, the manifold heat-control valve is mounted to the
    A. intake manifold   B cylinder head
    C. exhaust manifold   D. crankcase

KEY (CORRECT ANSWERS)

1.	D	11.	B
2.	C	12.	A
3.	A	13.	D
4.	C	14.	C
5.	B	15.	A
6.	D	16.	B
7.	C	17.	C
8.	C	18.	D
9.	B	19.	A
10.	A	20.	C

TEST 2

DIRECTIONS: Each question or incomplete statement is followed by several suggested answers or completions. Select the one that BEST answers the question or completes the statement. *PRINT THE LETTER OF THE CORRECT ANSWER IN THE SPACE AT THE RIGHT.*

1. When a ring ridge is removed from a cylinder, the BEST practice is to 1.____
   A. pull the piston from the cylinder before removing the ridge
   B. cut slightly below the level of the ridge into the cylinder
   C. blend the ridge area into the cylinder proper after removing the ridge
   D. leave a slight undercut in the cylinder wall after removing the ridge

2. The cleaning of ball and roller bearings is MOST effectively and safely 2.____
   accomplished by first wiping of surplus grease and oil and then
   A. soaking them in kerosene
   B. soaking them in gasoline
   C. soaking them in carbon-tetrachloride
   D. spinning them by using air pressure

3. The overheating of an engine would NOT likely be caused by 3.____
   A. a stuck manifold heat-control valve
   B. advanced ignition timing
   C. a lean carburetor mixture
   D. a leaking cylinder-head gasket

4. The excitation of the field of an automotive alternator is provided by current 4.____
   from the
   A. stator   B. rotor   C. diode   D. battery

5. A clicking or tapping noise which persists after the engine has warmed up is 5.____
   USUALLY
   A. loose fan belts   B. loose main bearings
   C. defective valve lifters D. worn piston pins

6. Compression piston rings for gasoline-powered engines are MOST generally 6.____
   made from
   A. copper   B. high-quality cast iron
   C. aluminum D. tempered steel

7. A vehicle has the coil spring mounted between the frame and the lower 7.____
   suspension arm.
   The front end ball joints on this vehicle may be checked by
   A. jacking up the lower suspension arm
   B. jacking up the frame
   C. blocking the upper suspension arm and jacking the frame
   D. jacking between the suspension arms

2 (#2)

8. The capacity of a conventional automobile ignition system condenser is MOST NEARLY
   A. 0.02 microfarads
   B. 0.2 microfarads
   C. 0.2 farads
   D. 2.0 farads

9. Of the following, the BEST sequence of operations to follow when removing grease and scale from carburetor and fuel pump parts would be
   A. degreasing soak, alkaline soak, water rinse, acid dip, hot water rise
   B. acid dip, degreasing soak, alkaline rinse, water rinse
   C. acid dip, water rinse, alkaline dip, water rinse, degreasing soak, water rinse
   D. acid dip, water rinse, alkaline dip, degreasing soak, acid rinse, water rinse

10. A ballast-type resistor in the primary circuit of a conventional automotive ignition system will
    A. deliver constant reduced voltage to the soil
    B. be bypassed at high engine speeds
    C. increase coil primary voltage at low engine speeds
    D. decrease in resistance value as its temperature increases

11. In order to minimize the coil load when installing a coil in an automobile in which the positive terminal of the battery is grounded, the coil should be wired with its
    A. *negative* terminal connected to the distributor
    B. *positive* terminal connected to the distributor
    C. *negative* terminal connected to the ground
    D. *positive* terminal connected to the positive battery terminal through the starter switch

12. Loose connecting-rod bearings are USUALLY indicated by a
    A. light rap or clatter when the engine is running with a light load at approximately 25 mph
    B. metallic rattle when the engine is idling unevenly
    C. clicking noise when the engine is cold
    D. sharp metallic double knock when the engine is idling

13. An ignition system is not functioning properly. In order to check the system, the high tension wire from the coil is held close to a ground at the same time as the ignition points are opened and closed.
    If a good spark occurs from the high tension wire to the ground, it would indicate that the problem is NOT with the
    A. motor
    B. condenser
    C. spark plug wires
    D. distributer cap

14. When an automotive generator regulator is adjusted, a 1/4 ohm resistor is inserted in the line from the batter terminal of the regulator to the battery. This permits adjustment to be made to the
    A. current regulator
    B. circuit breaker
    C. voltage regulator
    D. field relay

15. A tire showing excessive wear on one side of the tread indicate IMPROPER
    A. caster   B. camber   C. toe-in   D. tire pressure

16. Front wheel roller bearings should be adjusted to
    A. .001 to .003 inch end play
    B. .010 inch end play
    C. a 20-foot-pound torque on nut
    D. a mild pressure

17. In automotive air conditioning systems, the MOST commonly used refrigerant is
    A. dichlorodifluoromethane (12)
    B. carbon dioxide (CO_2)
    C. ammonia (NH_3)
    D. sulfur dioxide (SO_2)

18. In an automotive air conditioning system, the opening of the expansion valve is controlled PRIMARILY by the
    A. temperature within the vehicle
    B. evaporator temperature
    C. condenser temperature
    D. condenser pressure

19. When the front end of a vehicle with independent suspension is aligned, the front of the upper suspension arm is moved away from the center line of the vehicle.
    The adjustment will change
    A. the caster only, in the positive direction
    B. both the caster and the camber, in the positive direction
    C. both the caster and the camber, in the negative direction
    D. the caster in the positive direction and the camber in the negative direction

20. The vapor discharge valve in a diaphragm-type fuel pump normally
    A. controls pump discharge pressure
    B. is installed directly after the fuel outlet valve
    C. opens with rising fuel temperature
    D. is vented to the carburetor air cleaner to minimize pollution

KEY (CORRECT ANSWERS)

1. C	6. B	11. B	16. A
2. A	7. A	12. A	17. A
3. B	8. B	13. B	18. B
4. D	9. A	14. C	19. B
5. C	10. A	15. B	20. C

TEST 3

DIRECTIONS: Each question or incomplete statement is followed by several suggested answers or completions. Select the one that BEST answers the question or completes the statement. *PRINT THE LETTER OF THE CORRECT ANSWER IN THE SPACE AT THE RIGHT.*

1. In an automotive ignition system, the distributor dwell 1.____
   A. is governed by the ignition point gap
   B. is equal to 360 degrees divided by the number of cylinders
   C. is equal to the number of degrees of rotation that the points are open
   D. will decrease with increasing centrifugal advance

2. When an oscilloscope indicates too short a dwell in the ignition system, the MOST probable reason is that the 2.____
   A. points are set too far apart   B. points are set too close together
   C. degrees of dwell are too great D. coil output is too high

3. An automobile with a properly operating conventional assembly has one rear wheel jacked up. The engine is running in *drive* with 20 mph indicated on the speedometer. 3.____
   The MOST correct statement concerning this situation is that the
   A. vehicle will move off the jack because it has been driven by the wheel on the ground
   B. jacked rear wheel is turning at 20 mph road speed
   C. jacked rear wheel is turning at 40 mph road speed
   D. jacked rear wheel is turning at 10 mph road speed

4. Of the following tubing materials and connections, the BEST one to use when replacing hydraulic brake lines is 4.____
   A. steel tubing with compression fittings
   B. steel tubing with double-lap flare
   C. steel tubing with single-lap flare
   D. half hard copper tubing with double-lap flare

5. In a single-type brake master cylinder, a plugged compensating port would be suspected if 5.____
   A. the brakes drag
   B. the brake pedal is very low
   C. the brakes fade
   D. excessive pedal pressure is required

6. The PRIMARY purpose of the diverter valve in an AIR (Thermactor) emission control system is to 6.____
   A. prevent exhaust gases from reaching the pump
   B. cut off the flow of air to the exhaust manifold when the manifold pressure decreases suddenly

C. provide maximum ignition advance when decelerating in order to prevent backfiring
D. provide advance timing during prolonged idling

7. An automotive clutch throw-out bearing
   A. is mounted on the transmission input shaft
   B. is mounted on the transmission bearing retainer
   C. rotates when the clutch is engaged
   D. must be in continuous contact with the clutch release levers

8. An advantage of using a clutch that utilizes a diaphragm spring instead of coil spring is that such a clutch eliminates the need for
   A. a throw-out bearing   B. a pivot ring
   C. a throw-out fork   D. clutch release levers

9. Of the following statements concerning disc brakes, the one which is INCORRECT IS:
   A. All scoring of the disc must be ground out before the pads are replaced
   B. It is necessary to pump the brake pedal after changing the pads in order to make the brake function
   C. The piston seal automatically adjusts the pads to the disc clearance
   D. The run-out of the disc may not exceed .003"

10. Turning the carburetor idle aid adjusting screw outward will
    A. enrich the idle-air-fuel mixture
    B. lean the idle air-fuel mixture
    C. close down on the main throttle valve
    D. reduce the idle rpm

11. The function of an automotive choke vacuum break piston or diaphragm is to
    A. attempt to close the choke when the engine is accelerated
    B. apply an additional torque on the choke to assist the thermostatic spring in keeping the choke closed
    C. attempt to open the choke when the engine is accelerated
    D. act opposite to the incoming air pressure on the throat plate

12. A brake assembly has two single-ended cylinders, one on the top and one on the bottom. The opposite ends of the brake shoes are anchored to the backing plate.
    This type of brake would be considered as being
    A. a duo-servo   B. self-energizing
    C. self-centering   D. a uni-servo

13. An exhaust gas analyzer operating on the principle of thermal conductivity of the exhaust gas reads 12.0/1.0. This indicates that the
    A. mixture is lean
    B. mixture is rich
    C. carburetor setting conforms to Sec. 207 of the Federal Clean Air Act
    D. mixture has 12% excess air

14. When adjusting a recirculating ball, manual type, steering gear,
    A. the worm bearing preload adjustment should be made with the steering wheel in the *straight-ahead* position
    B. the pitman shaft preload adjustment should be made with the steering wheel in the *straight-ahead* position
    C. the pitman shaft preload should be made prior to worm bearing preload adjustments
    D. both worm bearing and pitman shaft preload adjustments should be made with the steering wheel one turn from the center

15. The device used in automatic transmissions to provide the force required to engage a band clutch is called a
    A. booster   B. shifter   C. spool   D. servo

16. The function of the governor valve in an automatic transmission NORMALLY is to
    A. maintain constant pressure in the control circuits
    B. provide proportionally increasing pressure to the shift valve as road speed increases
    C. provide pressure to the shift valve at a predetermined road speed
    D. increase band pressure during heavy acceleration

17. On many automatic transmissions, the function performed by the TV linkage is carried out by use of a
    A. vacuum modulator   B. servo
    C. dashpot   D. compensator valve

18. A centrifugal vacuum type of speed governor
    A. is mounted between the carburetor and intake manifold
    B. would not govern speed if the air lines were removed or tampered
    C. would close the throttle if the air lines were removed or tampered
    D. has a speed-control adjustment which is made at the carburetor

19. In an air brake system, a limiting quick release valve is NORMALLY found in
    A. the line to the front brake chamber
    B. the line to the rear brake chamber
    C. series with the trailer protection valve
    D. the governor control

20. Air-actuated brake shoes are adjusted by
    A. adjusting the length of the chamber piston rod
    B. shifting the brake chamber along the slotted holes in the mount
    C. moving the cam on the splined shaft
    D. rotating the camshaft to move the shoe closer to the brake drum

KEY (CORRECT ANSWERS)

1.	A	11.	A
2.	A	12.	B
3.	C	13.	A
4.	B	14.	B
5.	A	15.	D
6.	B	16.	C
7.	B	17.	A
8.	D	18.	B
9.	A	19.	A
10.	B	20.	D

EXAMINATION SECTION
TEST 1

DIRECTIONS: Each question or incomplete statement is followed by several suggested answers or completions. Select the one that BEST answers the question or completes the statement. *PRINT THE LETTER OF THE CORRECT ANSWER IN THE SPACE AT THE RIGHT.*

1. All of the following are probable causes of an engine's failure to start EXCEPT 1.____
   A. cylinders not wired in proper order
   B. poor coolant circulation
   C. resistance unit burned out
   D. defective condenser

2. In an *expert* system for offboard computer diagnosis, which stage of knowledge acquisition in developing problem-solving rules occurs FIRST? 2.____
   A. Implementation   B. Identification
   C. Formalization   D. Conceptualization

3. Some suspension units consist of tandem axles joined by a single cross support that also acts as a vertical pivot for the entire unit. 3.____
   These units are known as
   A. axials   B. field frames   C. bogies   D. helicals

4. In automotive electronics, the fractional duration that ignition points are closed is known as 4.____
   A. slip   B. gain   C. dwell   D. delay

5. A brake system's warning lights may be tested by 5.____
   A. testing the bulbs with an ohmmeter
   B. depressing the brake pedal and opening a wheel cylinder bleeder screw
   C. jumping the wires at the brake distributor switch assembly
   D. testing the system with an ammeter

6. Of the following procedures performed prior to grinding a valve seat, which should be performed FIRST? 6.____
   A. Reaming   B. Adjusting   C. Cleaning   D. Replacement

7. What type of clutch is responsible for controlling a car's air conditioning compressor? 7.____
   A. Centrifugal   B. Free-wheeling
   C. Magnetic   D. Mechanical

67

8. Which of the following is a DISADVANTAGE associated with onboard computer diagnostic systems?
   A. Inability to incorporate self-diagnosis
   B. Limited number of systems available for diagnosis
   C. Cannot be manually activated
   D. Inability to detect intermittent failures

9. Which parts in a motor or generator contact the rotating armature commutator or rings?
   A. Cams   B. Brushes   C. Rod caps   D. Bushings

10. What is the MAIN advantage associated with the use of offboard computer diagnostic systems?
    A. Decreased task load
    B. Continuous testing intervals
    C. Can be manually activated by the driver
    D. Capable of simultaneous multiple diagnoses

11. An EGO sensor used in a microprocessor-based control/diagnostic system
    A. is perfectly linear
    B. is unaffected by temperature
    C. has two different output levels, depending on the fuel mixture
    D. is unaffected by engine exhaust levels

12. To what drive train component is the ring gear in the differential bolted?
    A. Drive pinion   B. Axle shaft
    C. Differential case   D. Carrier

13. What is transmitted by the slip rings on an automotive alternator?
    A. Alternating current to the field coils
    B. Alternating current from the stator windings
    C. Direct current from the field coils
    D. Direct current to the alternator output terminals

14. Which of the following is a PROBABLE cause of an engine's missing at low speed?
    A. Poor compression   B. Leaky head gasket
    C. Carbon deposits in cylinders   D. Loose flywheel

15. In order for an onboard computer diagnostic system to detect a failure in the cars electronic system, the failure must be
    A. associated with engine performance
    B. intermittent
    C. symptomatic
    D. nonreversible

16. What is the term for the part of a shaft which rotates in a bearing?
    A. Lunette   B. Journal   C. Jackshaft   D. Kingpin

17. What is the USUAL steering gear reduction for passenger vehicles? ____-to-1.
    A. 2 B. 4 C. 8 D. 12

18. What is indicated by a low reading from 5 to 10 on an engine vacuum test?
    A. Broken piston ring
    B. Weak cylinders
    C. Late valve timing
    D. Valve sticking

19. Which of the following is NOT a component of the automotive power train?
    A. Steering gear
    B. Clutch
    C. Transmission
    D. Differential

20. Which instrument is NORMALLY used to check the condition of a resistance spark plug?
    A. Voltmeter B. Ohmmeter C. Ammeter D. Potentiometer

21. Which device is used to measure the resistance of a circuit or electrical machine?
    A. Ohmmeter B. Voltmeter C. Resistor D. Ammeter

22. What reading will appear on an infrared meter which indicates a failure of the catalytic converter? ____ HC/ ____ CO
    A. Low; high B. Low; low C. High; low D. High; high

23. In automatic transmissions, the servo
    A. operates the shifter valves
    B. applies the clutch
    C. applies the bands
    D. controls the output from the variable vane pump

24. If an onboard diagnostic system's fault code indicates that the O_2 sensor is not ready, all of the following are possible causes EXCEPT
    A. O_2 sensor is not functioning correctly
    B. defective connections or leads
    C. lack of O_2 contacting sensor
    D. control unit is not processing O_2 signal

25. The mechanical compressor in a car's air conditioning system is driven by
    A. an electric motor
    B. the axles
    C. the propeller shaft
    D. the crankshaft

KEY (CORRECT ANSWERS)

1.	B		11.	C
2.	B		12.	C
3.	C		13.	C
4.	C		14.	A
5.	B		15.	D
6.	C		16.	B
7.	C		17.	B
8.	D		18.	C
9.	B		19.	A
10.	A		20.	B

21. A
22. C
23. C
24. C
25. D

TEST 2

DIRECTIONS: Each question or incomplete statement is followed by several suggested answers or completions. Select the one that BEST answers the question or completes the statement. *PRINT THE LETTER OF THE CORRECT ANSWER IN THE SPACE AT THE RIGHT.*

1. When installing disc brake linings, a hammer should be used to 1.____
    A. tighten the shoe retainer
    B. seat the pads in the calipers
    C. shape the pads
    D. remove the linings

2. What engine component is lubricated by the oil squirt hole in the connecting rod? 2.____
    A. Connecting rod bearing
    B. Crankshaft
    C. Cylinder wall
    D. Piston pin

3. Which of the following is a PROBABLE cause of backfiring through a carburetor? 3.____
    A. Short circuit in switch
    B. Water in gasoline
    C. Overheating
    D. Sticky thermostat

4. What is the GREATEST danger associated with hydraulic braking systems? 4.____
    A. Uneven braking
    B. Defective metering valve
    C. Loss of brake fluid
    D. Dirty or clogged wheel cylinder

5. Under what conditions must an engine be operated during a cylinder balance test? 5.____
    A. With the spark plugs firing, one at a time, at 1500 rpm
    B. With all plugs shorted but two which fire at non-simultaneous equal intervals
    C. At idle speed, with all plugs shorted but two which fire at non-simultaneous equal intervals
    D. At idle speed, with the spark plugs shorted, one at a time

6. Which of the following is a requisite property of brake fluid? 6.____
    A. Has detergents for keeping hoses unobstructed
    B. High wetting characteristics
    C. High viscosity
    D. High boiling point and low freezing point

7. What is measured by the mass airflow sensor in a microprocessor-based control/diagnostic system? The 7.____
    A. rate at which air is flowing into an engine
    B. composition of a given mass of air
    C. rate at which exhaust is flowing out of an engine
    D. density of atmospheric air

8. What is placed at the joint of a steel frame in order to strengthen the joint? 8.____
    A. Wobble plate
    B. Gusset plate
    C. Jackshaft
    D. Lint pin

9. What is indicated if a combustion meter reading is 10% higher with the air cleaner in place than when the air cleaner has been removed?
   A. Clogged injectors
   B. Dirty air cleaner
   C. Clogged vent
   D. Normal operation

9.____

10. Which of the following is a PROBABLE cause of an engine failing to stop?
    A. Lack of pressure on gasoline tank
    B. Disconnected magneto ground
    C. High altitude
    D. Spark plug gaps too wide

10.____

11. Automotive sensors used in computer-operated diagnostic or control systems typically see changes in each of the following EXCEPT
    A. electrical signals
    B. temperature
    C. position
    D. pressure

11.____

12. What type of feeler gauge should be used to set the gap on a new set of spark plugs?
    A. Flat   B. Ramp-type   C. Wire   D. Round

12.____

13. Intake and exhaust manifolds are built with their walls contacting each other in order to
    A. reduce atomization
    B. pre-heat the fuel mixture
    C. facilitate valve action
    D. conserve space

13.____

14. Fuel tank vapors stored in the charcoal canister
    A. are released to the atmosphere through a bleed valve
    B. are released to the atmosphere through a port in the canister
    C. are cycled back into the fuel tank
    D. become part of the fuel mixture when the engine is started

14.____

15. The information handled by a computerized engine control system flows from
    A. computer to sensor to display
    B. actuator to display to computer
    C. sensor to computer to actuator
    D. sensor to display to computer

15.____

16. In a car with manual transmission, spring pressure clamps the friction disc between the pressure plate and the _____ when the clutch is engaged.
    A. sun gear
    B. reaction plate
    C. flywheel
    D. differential

16.____

17. If the insulation material used with a crimp connector on electric wiring is coded red, what range of gauges is considered typical?
    A. 10-12   B. 12-18   C. 14-16   D. 18-22

17.____

18. An air conditioning system's expansion valve controls the
    A. pressure of refrigerant in the compressor
    B. temperature of refrigerant in the condenser
    C. amount of refrigerant in the evaporator
    D. temperature of air in the car's interior

18.____

19. Each of the following is a probable cause of engine overheating EXCEPT
    A. slipping fan belt
    B. frozen radiator
    C. improper valve timing
    D. short circuit in distributor rotor

20. When using a short finder to trace a short circuit, which of the following steps should be performed LAST?
    A. Turn on all switches in a series with the circuit being tested
    B. Move the short finder meter along circuit wiring
    C. Remove the blown fuse while leaving the battery connected
    D. Connect the pulse unit of short finder across the fuse terminals

21. If a light load test is performed on a battery and the battery shows less than 1.95 volts in all cells, then the battery
    A. is overly discharged
    B. should be replaced
    C. needs charging
    D. is in good condition

22. A *thermistor* is a
    A. newly-developed type of transistor
    B. device for regulating engine temperature
    C. temperature control system operated by a car passenger
    D. semiconductor temperature sensor

23. An *expert* system for offboard computer diagnosis differs from other computerized diagnostic systems because it is capable of
    A. carrying out several diagnostic operations at once
    B. recommending repair procedures
    C. determining the causes of problems without manual assistance
    D. sensing faults in a circuitry that is not related to engine performance

24. In which type of engine are all valve contained in the cylinder block?
    A. V-type   B. Two-stroke   C. F-head   D. L-head

25. The function of a MAP sensor in a microprocessor-based control/diagnostic system is to
    A. sense anomalous changes in a vehicle's traveling direction
    B. measure changes in mean atmospheric pressure
    C. measure manifold absolute pressure
    D. measure fluctuations in manifold air flow

KEY (CORRECT ANSWERS)

1.	C		11.	A
2.	C		12.	C
3.	D		13.	B
4.	C		14.	D
5.	B		15.	C
6.	D		16.	C
7.	A		17.	D
8.	B		18.	C
9.	B		19.	C
10.	B		20.	B

21. A
22. D
23. B
24. D
25. C

TEST 3

DIRECTIONS: Each question or incomplete statement is followed by several suggested answers or completions. Select the one that BEST answers the question or completes the statement. *PRINT THE LETTER OF THE CORRECT ANSWER IN THE SPACE AT THE RIGHT.*

1. What is indicated by a sudden periodic drop of 1 or 2 points during a vacuum test on a car's engine? 1.____
   A. Spark plug failure
   B. Damaged distributor cap
   C. Coil failure
   D. Low oil pressure

2. A stud axle is articulated to an axle-beam or steering head by means of a 2.____
   A. journal   B. kingpin   C. gusset plate   D. poppet

3. Which of the following should be checked FIRST when examining a front suspension? 3.____
   A. Kingpins
   B. Steering connections
   C. Bumper and frame level
   D. Suspension arm pivots

4. Which of the following procedures involving a combustion efficiency tester will detect manifold leaks? 4.____
   A. Accelerating the engine to fast speed and checking for meter deflection
   B. Pumping the accelerator and checking for instant response in the combustion meter
   C. Applying a kerosene/oil mixture to the flange and manifold gaskets and checking for meter deflection
   D. Placing the engine on full choke and checking for meter deflection

5. If a car's battery is always fully charged, which of the following should be checked? 5.____
   A. Short circuiting in alternator
   B. Output amperage of the alternator
   C. volt regulator output
   D. Volt regulator points

6. Which of the following are companion cylinders in a car's V-8 engine? 6.____
   A. 1 and 8   B. 2 and 8   C. 3 and 4   D. 2 and 7

7. Which of the following is a PROBABLE cause of firing in a car's muffler? 7.____
   A. Too rich a fuel mixture
   B. Carbon deposits in cylinder
   C. Improperly adjusted valve tappets
   D. Water in gasoline

8. What is the MAJOR benefit associated with the use of *expert* offboard computer diagnostic systems? 8.____
   A. High task load capability
   B. Continuous testing intervals
   C. Consistent application of problem-solving strategies
   D. Simultaneous multiple-system capability

9. Which type of valve is used to sense how fast a vehicle is traveling?
   A. Throttle   B. Governor   C. Manual   D. Modulator

10. A two-unit alternator is composed of a
    A. voltage limiter and current limiter
    B. current limiter and reverse current relay
    C. voltage limiter and field relay
    D. current limiter and field relay

11. Which type of gears are used for the forward speeds of fully synchronized standard transmissions?
    A. Helical
    B. Double helical
    C. Hypoid
    D. Spur

12. When checking a circuit for voltage drop, which of the following steps should be performed FIRST?
    A. Select the voltmeter range just above the battery circuit
    B. Connect the positive lead of the voltmeter to the end of the wire closest to the battery
    C. Connect the negative lead of the voltmeter to the end of the wire farthest from the battery
    D. Switch on the circuit

13. Each of the following is a probable cause of engine knocking EXCEPT
    A. compression too low
    B. loose piston
    C. spark too far advanced
    D. engine overheated

14. In what portion of an *expert* system for offboard computer diagnosis are logical operation performed?
    A. Domain
    B. Inference engine
    C. Knowledge base
    D. Interface

15. In the propeller shaft of an automotive transmission, a universal joint allows variation in the
    A. speed of rotation
    B. angle of drive
    C. length of the shaft
    D. direction of rotation

16. Which of the following is a POSSIBLE use for an engine analyzer?
    A. Setting the choke
    B. Measuring intake fuel flow rate
    C. Setting ignition points
    D. Measuring fuel mixture

17. What is the term for the smaller of two mating or meshing gears?
    A. Linch   B. Master   C. Pinion   D. Pilot

18. Conditioned air in an automotive air conditioning system is cooled as it passes through the
    A. condenser   B. evaporator   C. compressor   D. receiver

19. In order to determine the correct valve timing of an engine, the opening and closing of the valves should be measured in reference to the
    A. cylinder compression ratio
    B. fuel mixing jets
    C. distributor setting
    D. piston position

    19.____

20. In modern engines using computer-based control systems, diagnosis is performed
    A. with an engine analyzer
    B. with a timing light only
    C. with a timing light and voltmeter
    D. in the digital control system

    20.____

21. What is the MOST probable cause of a car drifting from side to side on a level road?
    A. Bent steering arm
    B. Tight shock absorber
    C. Loose steering connections
    D. Bent axle

    21.____

22. Which device, as part of a special type of pump, drives plunger back and forth as it rotates, producing the pumping action?
    A. Trunnion
    B. Torus
    C. Camber link
    D. Wobble plate

    22.____

23. In a microprocessor-based control/diagnostic system, a typical engine crankshaft angular position sensor is MOST effectively located on the
    A. camshaft
    B. crankshaft
    C. compressor pulley
    D. flywheel

    23.____

24. Which type of gauge will allow a mechanic to MOST accurately set the proper electrode gap on a spark plug?
    A. Flat feeler
    B. Round wire feeler
    C. Square wire feeler
    D. Dial

    24.____

25. What type of logical rule bases are programmed into MOST expert diagnostic systems?
    A. Either/or
    B. Set/subset
    C. If/then
    D. Inductive

    25.____

KEY (CORRECT ANSWERS)

1. A
2. B
3. C
4. C
5. C

6. B
7. A
8. C
9. B
10. C

11. A
12. B
13. A
14. B
15. B

16. C
17. C
18. B
19. D
20. D

21. C
22. D
23. B
24. B
25. C

EXAMINATION SECTION
TEST 1

DIRECTIONS: Each question or incomplete statement is followed by several suggested answers or completions. Select the one that BEST answers the question or completes the statement. *PRINT THE LETTER OF THE CORRECT ANSWER IN THE SPACE AT THE RIGHT.*

1. A mechanic who discovers that the friction-disc facing of a dry clutch is saturated with oil should
    A. use a heavier oil
    B. wash the facing in solvent
    C. replace the facing
    D. increase clutch spring pressure

    1.____

2. Which of the following steps, performed prior to the removal of a transmission oil cooler, should occur FIRST?
    A. Removal of transmission case
    B. Removal of valve body assembly
    C. Checking transmission fluid level
    D. Draining radiator

    2.____

3. An alternator voltage regulator controls alternator output by
    A. grounding the negative diodes
    B. grounding the stator windings
    C. controlling the voltage output at the B terminal
    D. controlling the current feed to the rotor

    3.____

4. Which clutch part is located between the engine flywheel and the pressure plate?
    A. Release lever
    B. Fork
    C. Friction disc
    D. Adjusting screw

    4.____

5. In a digital microcomputer used for the control or diagnosis of automotive engine, some device is needed to convert the computer's output data into a form readable by people.
    The component which serve this function are known as
    A. data buses
    B. microprocessors
    C. peripherals
    D. accumulators

    5.____

6. What is being adjusted when a mechanic pulls the entire control arm toward the frame?
    A. Caster
    B. Camber
    C. Tracking
    D. Kingpin inclination

    6.____

7. Which of the following is a characteristic that could NOT typically be identified by a onboard computer diagnostic system?
    A. Faulty EGR circuits
    B. The cause of a short circuit
    C. Low ECT input
    D. Lean fuel mixture

    7.____

8. In an automatic transmission, the oil filter is USUALLY secured by means of
   A. screws or a clip
   B. the oil pan
   C. a bracket assembly
   D. a spring

9. In a microprocessor-based control/diagnostic system, which type of actuator recirculates exhaust gas to the intake charge?
   A. Fuel metering   B. Ignition   C. EGR   D. EGO

10. Which of the following is a PROBABLE cause of an engine's missing at high speed?
    A. Carbon deposits in cylinder
    B. Scored cylinder
    C. Short circuit in distributor rotor
    D. Weak valve spring

11. Which of the following operations is performed by a sensor in a microprocessor-based control/diagnostic system?
    A. Sending signals to the driver
    B. Selecting the transmission gear ratio
    C. Measuring variables in physical qualities
    D. Serving as an output device

12. When a hydraulic brake pedal is released quickly, the initial makeup fluid is supplied to the master cylinder's pressure chamber through the
    A. piston bleeder holes
    B. compensating port
    C. check valve
    D. port holes

13. Which part of a transaxle drives the output shafts?
    A. Ring gear assembly
    B. Pinion gears
    C. Side gears
    D. Chain

14. Which of the following problems would be MOST difficult to solve with an onboard computer diagnostic system?
    A. Air pump switching valve failure
    B. Imbalanced injectors
    C. Fuel pump circuit fault
    D. Defective electronic spark timing circuit

15. What is the MOST likely cause of a buzzing noise in the automatic transmission?
    A. Vacuum leakage
    B. Malfunctioning front pump
    C. Bent pilot shaft
    D. Worn clutch plates

16. What is the function of an actuator in a microprocessor-based control/diagnostic system?
    A. Indicates results of a measurement
    B. Creates a response to an electrical signal
    C. Serves as an input device
    D. Provides a mathematical model for an engine

17. The constant flow method of fuel injection places its burden on each of the following components EXCEPT
    A. an engine-driven injection pump equipped with plungers
    B. injector nozzles
    C. metering valve
    D. bypass unit

18. Which device is used specifically to regulate current by means of variable resistance?
    A. Capacitor   B. Rheostat   C. Ohmmeter   D. Volute

19. Which type of spring is used in a spring-loaded disc clutch?
    A. Cantilever   B. Volute   C. Helical   D. Diaphragm

20. When the engine is running, power steering fluid travels from
    A. control valve to reservoir to pump
    B. pump to control valve to reservoir
    C. reservoir to pump to control valve
    D. reservoir to control valve to pump

21. Piezoresistivity is
    A. a resistance property of insulators
    B. a property of certain semiconductors in which resistivity varies with strain
    C. the ratio of resistivity in a semiconductor to the property being measured by a sensor
    D. a type of metal bonding pad

22. Which of the following would be a PROBABLE cause of engine stoppage?
    A. Fuel pump breakdown   B. Disconnected magneto ground
    C. High altitude   D. Blown cylinder-head gasket

23. If the insulation material used with a crimp connector on electric wiring is coded yellow, what range of gauges is considered typical?
    A. 10-12   B. 12-18   C. 14-16   D. 18-22

24. What is the MOST common firing order of an in-line 6-cylinder engine?
    A. 1-6-2-5-3-4   B. 1-3-6-4-2-5   C. 1-2-5-6-3-4   D. 1-5-3-6-2-4

25. The pressure sensor of most fuel injection systems is located
    A. in the injection chamber
    B. at the nozzle port
    C. within the pump housing
    D. beneath the floor, at the side of the engine compartment

KEY (CORRECT ANSWERS)

1. C
2. D
3. C
4. C
5. C

6. B
7. B
8. A
9. C
10. D

11. C
12. D
13. C
14. A
15. B

16. B
17. A
18. B
19. A
20. B

21. C
22. A
23. A
24. D
25. D

TEST 2

DIRECTIONS: Each question or incomplete statement is followed by several suggested answers or completions. Select the one that BEST answers the question or completes the statement. *PRINT THE LETTER OF THE CORRECT ANSWER IN THE SPACE AT THE RIGHT.*

1. What is the term for a spring-loaded ball that engages a notch? 1.____
   A. Roller bearing   B. Poppet   C. Venturi   D. Lunette

2. What changes alternating current to direct current in the alternator? 2.____
   A. Field relay
   B. Stator windings
   C. Rotor slip rings
   D. Diodes

3. If a mechanic is using an expert diagnostic system and encounters no rules in the conflict set, what should be done? 3.____
   A. Use highest-priority rules for predicted condition
   B. Stop the procedure
   C. Use the rule that most commonly appears under similar conditions
   D. Switch to a different database

4. With which drive train component does a transmission's reverse idler gear ALWAYS mesh? 4.____
   A. Clutch plate
   B. Second gear
   C. Countershaft reverse gear
   D. Main shaft reverse gear

5. Which of the following is the MOST probable cause for a noise that is present in the rear end only when a car goes around curves? 5.____
   A. Loose universal joint
   B. Trouble in the differential case assembly
   C. Trouble in the drive-pinion assembly
   D. Dry wheel bearing

6. In a microprocessor-based control/diagnostic system, which type of sensor is basically a resistor with a movable contact? 6.____
   A. Crankshaft position
   B. Throttle angle
   C. EGO
   D. Knock

7. What is being indicated by bubbles in an air conditioning sight gauge if the unit has been running for several minutes? 7.____
   A. Low refrigerant
   B. Low compressor pressure
   C. System leakage
   D. Normal operation

8. When checking connecting rods for alignment, the angle the rod aligner mandrel makes with the face plate should be _____ degrees, depending on the type of jig used. 8.____
   A. 10 or 20   B. 45 or 90   C. 90 or 180   D. 180 or 320

83

9. Which type of fuel injection system typically sprays fuel into each intake port on the manifold side of the intake valve?
   A. Direct
   B. Port
   C. Sequential
   D. Single-point

10. The purpose of a suction throttling valve used in an automotive air conditioning system is to
    A. prevent freezing in the evaporator
    B. control compressor cycles
    C. control the metering of the expansion valve
    D. maintain low condenser pressure

11. In a microprocessor-based control/diagnostic system, which type of actuator consists of a spray nozzle and a solenoid-operated plunger?
    A. Thermostat
    B. Ignition
    C. EGO
    D. Fuel injector

12. Which component of a band and servo assembly is DIRECTLY affected by hydraulic pressure?
    A. Anchor
    B. Band
    C. Servo piston
    D. Stem

13. If an ammeter shows a small fluctuating reading and a spark test reveals no spark, what is the MOST likely source of the trouble?
    A. Primary circuit
    B. Secondary circuit
    C. Battery
    D. Ignition switch

14. All of the following are characteristics of a top-feed fuel injector, as opposed to a bottom-feed EXCEPT
    A. uses incoming air for cooling purposes
    B. higher cost
    C. greater pressure requirements
    D. heavier mass

15. All of the following are probable causes of an engine's lacking power EXCEPT
    A. too rich a fuel mixture
    B. lack of coolant
    C. high altitude
    D. leaky manifold gaskets

16. Which device should be used to check for runout or wobble on a disc brake that has been lathe-mounted?
    A. Timing light
    B. Electric meter
    C. Dial indicator
    D. Torque wrench

17. A(n) _____ is the term for a wire or wires that form a common path to and from the various components a microcomputer uses for the diagnosis or control of an automotive engine.
    A. analog
    B. runner
    C. bus
    D. port

18. The notch on the head of a piston should be facing the _____ during the installation of a piston assembly.
    A. minor thrust side
    B. major thrust side
    C. rear of the engine
    D. front of the engine

19. The requisite knowledge and expertise used in an expert diagnostic system's programming is acquired from a person known as the
    A. domain expert
    B. user
    C. inference engine
    D. knowledge engineer

20. All of the following are probable causes of an engine's missing at all speeds EXCEPT
    A. valve tappets adjusted too closely
    B. dirty plug
    C. loose piston
    D. leak in intake manifold

21. The function of a MAP sensor in a microprocessor-based control/diagnostic system is to measure
    A. anomalous changes in a vehicle's traveling direction
    B. changes in mean atmospheric pressure
    C. manifold absolute pressure
    D. fluctuations in manifold air flow

22. What procedure is recommended upon discovering that brake fluid is contaminated?
    A. Bleed the hydraulic system
    B. Flush the system with alcohol, and then adding clean fluid
    C. Add a detergent oil to the system
    D. Replace the fluid, along with all hydraulic rubber cups and seals

23. Which of the following could be indicated by a vibrating reading on a vacuum gauge that appears only at high engine speeds?
    A. Pitted distributor points
    B. Incorrect ignition timing
    C. Blow-by
    D. Weak valve springs

24. In a microprocessor-based control/diagnostic system, which type of sensor uses magnetostrictive techniques?
    A. Knock
    B. Throttle angle
    C. EGO
    D. MAP

25. The amount that the steering knuckle pivots are angled away from a true vertical is known as
    A. camber
    B. phase
    C. tilt
    D. caster

KEY (CORRECT ANSWERS)

1.	B		11.	D
2.	D		12.	C
3.	B		13.	B
4.	C		14.	A
5.	C		15.	D
6.	B		16.	C
7.	A		17.	C
8.	C		18.	D
9.	B		19.	D
10.	A		20.	C

21. C
22. D
23. D
24. A
25. D

TEST 3

DIRECTIONS: Each question or incomplete statement is followed by several suggested answers or completions. Select the one that BEST answers the question or completes the statement. *PRINT THE LETTER OF THE CORRECT ANSWER IN THE SPACE AT THE RIGHT.*

1. All of the following are components of a positive crankcase ventilating system EXCEPT the 1.____
   A. manifold suction tube
   B. metering valve
   C. road draft tube
   D. intake breather

2. The MAXIMUM voltage for sensor and actuator circuits used in onboard diagnostic systems is 2.____
   A. 3 B. 5 C. 10 D. 15

3. Which of the following is a PROBABLE result of adjusting valves with too little clearance? 3.____
   A. Delayed timing
   B. Burning oil
   C. Lower fuel economy
   D. Overheated valves

4. In a fuel metering actuator that is used in a microprocessor-based control/diagnostic system, *duty cycle* refers too the ratio of fuel 4.____
   A. *off* time to fuel *on* time
   B. *on* time to fuel *off* time
   C. *on* time to fuel *on* time plus fuel *off* time
   D. *off* time to fuel *off* time pus fuel *on* time

5. In a synchromesh transmission, gears are engaged by a _____ in order to prevent gear clashing. 5.____
   A. slip joint or spline
   B. friction and dog clutch
   C. planetary unit
   D. dog clutch

6. An EGO sensor is a 6.____
   A. device for measuring the oxygen concentration in automotive engine exhaust
   B. spark plug advance mechanism
   C. device for measuring crankshaft acceleration
   D. device for measuring the concentrations of various exhaust gases

7. What type of expander must be used under an oil ring? 7.____
   A. Step joint
   B. Diagonal joint
   C. Rigid
   D. Vented

8. Which of the following procedures is included in the performance of a compression test on a car engine? 8.____
   A. Perform entire test while engine is cold
   B. Test one cylinder at a time, with the corresponding plug temporarily removed

87

C. Crank for no more than two compression strokes
D. Block open throttle and choke

9. Air enters most Bosch electronic fuel injection systems through the
   A. oil bath cleaner
   B. injector choke
   C. compressor line
   D. injector manifold

9.____

10. The idler arm is attached to the _____ in a typical steering mechanism
    A. center link   B. tie rod   C. pitman arm   D. spindle

10.____

11. In a microprocessor-based control/diagnostic system, which type of crankshaft position sensor uses a disk having several holes?
    A. Optical
    B. Ignition timing
    C. Hall-effect
    D. Magnetic reluctance

11.____

12. In a mechanical fuel pump, pressure is maintained by means of
    A. a spring under the diaphragm
    B. a motor
    C. a needle valve
    D. rotating vanes

12.____

13. If a third pump is used in a fuel injection system, it is mounted
    A. on the fuel tank pump pickup tube
    B. in the line between the pickup tube and the pressure pump
    C. in the line between the pressure pump and fuel metering assembly
    D. at the fuel metering assembly

13.____

14. Which part of a cooling system thermostat opens and closes system valves?
    A. Pressure valve
    B. Vacuum valve
    C. Bellows
    D. Seater

14.____

15. What is the term for the front portion of a vehicle body or cab which partially encloses the dash panel and forms the windshield frame?
    A. Cowl   B. Hull   C. Head   D. Mask

15.____

16. How many digits make up a fault code used in a typical onboard computer diagnostic system?
    A. 1   B. 2   C. 3   D. 4

16.____

17. Which of the following should be checked FIRST when all brakes are dragging?
    A. Brake fluid level
    B. Master cylinder compensating port
    C. Wheel cylinders
    D. Brake pedal free travel

17.____

18. Which type of sensor measure is NOT capable of measuring the amount of air flowing through a fuel injection system?
    A. Speed-density
    B. Plate
    C. Differential
    D. Mass airflow

18.____

19. Which type of engine contains valves both in the head and the cylinder block?
    A. V-type   B. Two-stroke   C. F-head   D. L-head

19.____

20. Toe-in adjustments made by turning the adjusting sleeves on the tie rods in equal amounts in opposite directions are done to
    A. keep the wheels in balance
    B. keep the steering wheel centered
    C. avoid over-adjustment
    D. prevent excessive steering wheel play

21. Which of the following is NOT a possible cause of an overly lean fuel mixture that appears during a no-load carburetor mixture test?
    A. Plugged metering jets   B. Stuck float
    C. Bad metering rod adjustment   D. Manifold air leak

22. Which of the following is NOT a component of a pressure regulator used in fuel injection systems?
    A. Spring   B. Manifold   C. Diaphragm   D. Valve

23. During installation of the transmission, _____ can be used to turn the drive plate in order to connect it with the converter.
    A. the transmission unit   B. the cranking motor
    C. the output shaft   D. a wrench

24. Which type of bearing is NOT used on automotive drive axles?
    A. Sleeve   B. Roller   C. Taper   D. Ball

25. What is the term for the action or process of producing voltage by the relative motion of a magnetic field and a conductor?
    A. Induction   B. Resistance
    C. Condensation   D. Conduction

KEY (CORRECT ANSWERS)

1.	C		11.	A
2.	B		12.	A
3.	D		13.	D
4.	C		14.	C
5.	B		15.	A
6.	A		16.	B
7.	B		17.	D
8.	D		18.	C
9.	A		19.	C
10.	A		20.	B

21. C
22. B
23. B
24. A
25. A

EXAMINATION SECTION

TEST 1

DIRECTIONS: Each question or incomplete statement is followed by several suggested answers or completions. Select the one that BEST answers the question or completes the statement. *PRINT THE LETTER OF THE CORRECT ANSWER IN THE SPACE AT THE RIGHT.*

1. All of the following are probable sources of drivability problems EXCEPT the   1.____
   A. battery system   B. engine condition
   C. ignition system   D. fuel delivery system

2. Bending the _____ is the BEST way to adjust the ignition point contact.   2.____
   A. movable point arm   B. breaker plate
   C. stationary point bracket   D. pivot post

3. If an ignition system's breaker points are pitted, what should a mechanic check FIRST?   3.____
   A. Distributor condenser   B. Distributor cap
   C. Circuit breaker   D. Coil

4. Which cooling system component should be checked if a car's air conditioning blower operates properly but system output is still inadequate?   4.____
   A. Receiver-drier   B. Evaporator core
   C. Temperature control   D. Condenser

5. Excessive wear of brake linings will MOST likely cause   5.____
   A. stiff pedal   B. drum scoring
   C. sticky wheel   D. drag on brakes

6. The PCV valve is connected between the   6.____
   A. transmission and clutch   B. injector and fuel pump
   C. exhaust pipe and intake manifold   D. crankcase and intake manifold

7. What device is MOST effective for checking fuel pump performance?   7.____
   A. Vacuum switch   B. Micrometer
   C. Voltmeter   D. Stethoscope prod

8. For what purpose are the points of a conventional ignition system adjusted to increase the point gap? To   8.____
   A. advance the ignition timing
   B. increase the dwell angle
   C. decrease the dwell angle with no change in timing
   D. slow the ignition timing

9. Which of the following is NOT a type of temperature sensor used in microprocessor-based control/diagnostic systems?
   A. Wire-wound resistor
   B. Potentiometer
   C. Semiconductor resistor
   D. Thermistor

10. The various relationships and fundamental data associated with the use of an expert diagnostic system are known as the
    A. domain
    B. inference engine
    C. knowledge base
    D. interface

11. Which type of electric starting motor is often used because of its high starting torque?
    A. Compound-wound
    B. Shunt-wound
    C. Series-wound
    D. Capacitor

12. The auto system that is LEAST likely to cause engine operating problems is the _____ system.
    A. starting
    B. charging
    C. ignition
    D. fuel injection

13. Which device is capable of measuring volts, ohms, and amperes in solid-state electronic equipment?
    A. Digital multimeter
    B. Analog multimeter
    C. Jumper wires
    D. Continuity tester

14. Which of the following is a PROBABLE cause of backfiring in an intake manifold?
    A. Broken connecting rod
    B. Incorrect valve timing
    C. Sticky choke valve
    D. A lean cold-engine fuel mixture

15. An EGO sensor that is used in a microprocessor-based control/diagnostic system should NOT be used for control at a temperature less than _____ °C.
    A. 0
    B. 100
    C. 200
    D. 300

16. What is the PROBABLE result of setting a spark plug gap more closely than normal?
    A. Smoother idling
    B. Hard starting
    C. Easier starting
    D. Rougher idling

17. Adjusting the _____ will help the steering of a car return to a straight position after cornering.
    A. toe-in
    B. toe-out
    C. caster
    D. camber

18. What is the basic work register in microcomputers that is used for automotive engine control an diagnostics?
    A. Status register
    B. Condition code register
    C. Brancher
    D. Accumulator

19. A car lacks power and a popping sound can be heard. 19.____
    What is the MOST likely cause?
    A. Shorted spark plug
    B. Uneven fuel supply
    C. Pitted breaker points
    D. Bad distributor timing

20. What is the term for the reinforcing ridge around a tire opening where it fits 20.____
    the wheel rim?
    A. Piping　　B. Binder　　C. Ram　　D. Bead

21. When checking a circuit for voltage drop, which of the following steps 21.____
    should be performed LAST?
    A. Select the voltmeter range just above the battery circuit
    B. Connect the positive lead of the voltmeter to the end of the wire closest to the battery
    C. Connect the negative lead of the voltmeter to the end of the wire farthest from the battery
    D. Switch on the circuit

22. If a battery frequently needs recharging, all of the following are probable 22.____
    causes EXCEPT
    A. poorly sized alternator drive pulley
    B. cell leakage
    C. poorly grounded voltage regulator
    D. sulfated battery

23. The diagnosis of intermittent failures in computer-based engine control systems 23.____
    is
    A. readily found using standard service bay equipment
    B. accomplished by displaying fault codes to the driver at the time of the failure
    C. sometimes accomplished by means of warning lamps on the dash display
    D. routinely accomplished with the onboard diagnostic capability of the control system

24. Before disassembling an air-release parking brake, it is necessary to FIRST 24.____
    A. remove the diaphragm clamp
    B. remove the quick release valve
    C. compress the apply spring
    D. fill the air reservoir

25. What is the MOST probable result of incorrect camber on car wheels? 25.____
    A. Abnormal tire wear along one side of the tread
    B. Damaged shocks
    C. Front-end shimmy
    D. Pulling to the side while braking

KEY (CORRECT ANSWERS)

1.	A	11.	C
2.	C	12.	D
3.	A	13.	A
4.	C	14.	D
5.	B	15.	D
6.	D	16.	D
7.	D	17.	B
8.	A	18.	D
9.	B	19.	B
10.	C	20.	D

21.	D
22.	B
23.	C
24.	C
25.	A

TEST 2

DIRECTIONS: Each question or incomplete statement is followed by several suggested answers or completions. Select the one that BEST answers the question or completes the statement. *PRINT THE LETTER OF THE CORRECT ANSWER IN THE SPACE AT THE RIGHT.*

1. The fuel pump in MOST fuel injection systems operates when the engine has oil pressure, and when the cranking speed is above _____ rpm.   1.____
    A. 50-75   B. 150-200   C. 500-1000   D. 1000-2000

2. What is indicated by an occasional 3-4 inch drop in a vacuum gauge test?   2.____
    A. Slowed timing
    B. Carburetor failure
    C. Valve sticking
    D. Incorrectly gapped plugs

3. All of the following are types of compressors used in automotive air conditioning systems EXCEPT   3.____
    A. 90-degree V
    B. 2-cylinder in-line
    C. axial
    D. hermetically sealed

4. How much free action does a mechanic typically allow in the brake pedal?   4.____
    A. None   B. 1/8 inch   C. 1/4 inch   D. 1/2 inch

5. Tire wear that is concentrated on both sides of the tread is USUALLY the result of   5.____
    A. toe-out
    B. improper balance
    C. over-inflation
    D. under-inflation

6. Temperature sensors that are a part of microprocessor-based electronic control/diagnostic systems use a type of semiconductor to measure temperature.   6.____
    The resistance of this semiconductor
    A. is always 100,000 ohms
    B. varies in direct proportion to temperature
    C. varies in inverse proportion to temperature
    D. varies in direct proportion to engine speed

7. Using a test lamp across the breaker points, and with the ignition switch on, a mechanic will rotate the _____ to obtain the correct timing.   7.____
    A. distributor housing until the light goes out
    B. distributor housing until the light goes on
    C. engine until the light goes out
    D. engine until the light goes on

8. In constant-flow fuel injection systems, pressure and circulation are provided by a(n)   8.____
    A. injection pump
    B. hydraulic line
    C. engine-driven rotary pump
    D. bellows

9. Which of the following could NOT be determined by using an armature growler to test a starting motor armature?
   A. Insulation condition
   B. Location of short circuits
   C. Amount of resistance
   D. Commutator condition

10. What is measured by the crankcase angular position sensor in a microprocessor-based control/diagnostic system? The
    A. oil pressure angle
    B. angle between a line drawn through a crankshaft axis, a mark on the flywheel, and a reference line
    C. angle between the connecting rods and the crankshaft
    D. pitch angle of the crankshaft

11. If the insulation material used with a crimp conector on electric wiring is coded blue, what range of gauges is considered typical?
    A. 10-12   B. 12-18   C. 14-16   D. 18-22

12. Which type of pump is used ONLY as a supply pump in some fuel injection systems?
    A. Rotary   B. Diaphragm   C. Turbine   D. Roller

13. In what part of a car's air conditioning system does the refrigerant lose heat?
    A. Receiver   B. Compressor   C. Condenser   D. Evaporator

14. When disc brake pads are retracted so as not to make contact with the rotor surface, the amount of retraction
    A. is limited by the metering valve
    B. must be a minimum of 1/16 inch
    C. is affected by the piston return springs
    D. is affected by the piston seals

15. What is the term for the high curved portion of a cam that produce maximum valve lift?
    A. Peak
    B. Nose circle
    C. Flank circle
    D. Radial circle

16. The current from a battery generally flows to the alternator _____ when a vehicle is started?
    A. rectifier
    B. rotor winding
    C. stator windings
    D. commutator

17. If the cam dwell angle of a distributor is less than the specified minimum, it is LIKELY that the
    A. rubbing block will wear down
    B. distributor contact points will become pitted
    C. ignition coil output will increase at high engine speeds
    D. ignition timing will be off

18. The ignition quality of diesel fuel is measured against an index known as the
    A. lean parameter
    B. cetane rating
    C. atomization ratio
    D. vortex flow chart

19. During timing operations on a six-cylinder engine, a timing light should be connected to spark plug number
    A. 6
    B. 4
    C. 2
    D. 1

20. In a microprocessor-based control/diagnostic system, which type of actuator serves to lower NO emissions?
    A. Ignition
    B. Fuel metering
    C. EGR
    D. EGO

21. What is indicated by a faintly vibrating needle during an engine vacuum test?
    A. Weak cylinders
    B. Leaking valves
    C. Obstruction in the exhaust system
    D. A broken piston ring

22. Which of the following components is NOT carried by a car's wheel knuckle assembly?
    A. Disc brake caliper mounting
    B. Rotor
    C. Steering arm
    D. Drum backing plate

23. If a mechanic hears a squealing noise during operation after the installation of an automatic transmission, what is the MOST likely source of the trouble?
    A. Rear bearing
    B. Regulator body mating surfaces
    C. Speedometer pinion
    D. Front pump drive sleeve or pump pinion

24. How should a mechanic decrease ignition point dwell?
    A. Rotate distributor body in the direction opposite the distributor shaft rotation
    B. Install weaker springs in the advance unit
    C. Increase the point gap
    D. Decrease the point gap

25. Before charging a battery, the battery ground cable should be disconnected at the battery.
    This is done in order to protect the
    A. alternator regulator
    B. alternator diodes
    C. ignition coil
    D. ignition module

KEY (CORRECT ANSWERS)

1.	B		11.	C
2.	C		12.	C
3.	D		13.	C
4.	C		14.	D
5.	D		15.	B
6.	C		16.	B
7.	B		17.	D
8.	C		18.	B
9.	C		19.	D
10.	B		20.	C

21. A
22. B
23. D
24. A
25. B

TEST 3

DIRECTIONS: Each question or incomplete statement is followed by several suggested answers or completions. Select the one that BEST answers the question or completes the statement. *PRINT THE LETTER OF THE CORRECT ANSWER IN THE SPACE AT THE RIGHT.*

1. Against what part of a bearing do rollers or balls move? 1.____
   A. Sleeve   B. Spread   C. Knuckle   D. Race

2. All of the following are desirable characteristics of an EGO sensor used in a microprocessor-based electronic control/diagnostic system EXCEPT 2.____
   A. variable voltages with respect to exhaust temperature
   B. rapid switching of output voltage in response to exhaust gas oxygen changes
   C. abrupt change in voltage at the optimal combustion ratio
   D. large difference in sensor output voltage between rich and lean mixture conditions

3. A _____ joint is used to allow changes in the length of a propeller shaft. 3.____
   A. slip   B. shaft   C. universal   D. idler

4. Which of the following should be adjusted LAST in performing a tune-up on a car with a carburetor? 4.____
   A. Drive belts   B. Manifold heat control valve
   C. Carburetor   D. EGR valve

5. What device operates the plungers in a fuel injection pump? 5.____
   A. Pump camshaft   B. Belt
   C. Engine camshaft   D. Drive chain

6. Ignition of the combustion charge before the spark has formed across the plug electrodes is known as 6.____
   A. cold firing   B. knocking
   C. backfiring   D. preignition

7. Gear-train end play can be adjusted by 7.____
   A. changing the snap ring
   B. removing the clutch plates and installing retainer ring
   C. changing the selective thrust washer
   D. installing different pinion carriers

8. Unlike a conventional spark plug, a resistor plug will 8.____
   A. require higher voltage to function
   B. lengthen the capacitive part of the spark
   C. shrink the inductive part of the spark
   D. have an auxiliary air gap

99

9. Which measuring device is used MAINLY to check for voltage in a circuit while power is connected to the circuit?
   A. Digital multimeter
   B. Jumper wires
   C. Test lights
   D. Short finder

10. The flexible link that allows a suspension spring's length to change as it flexes is the
    A. shackle
    B. strut
    C. flange
    D. trailing arm

11. What type of electrical connectors are generally used with component that are occasionally disconnected?
    A. Crimp
    B. Bullet
    C. Butt
    D. Snap-splice

12. Which of the following device is NOT appropriate for checking the distributor automatic advance operations?
    A. Tachometer
    B. Voltmeter
    C. Vacuum pump
    D. Timing light

13. Engine bearings are commonly made from each of the following materials EXCEPT
    A. babbit
    B. case-hardened steel
    C. aluminum
    D. copper-lead mix

14. What should be used with bolts or screws on bearing surface designed to retain end thrust?
    A. Toggles
    B. Plain washers
    C. Thrust washers
    D. Lock washers

15. An automotive technician's basic measurement tool is the
    A. dial gauge
    B. feeler gauge
    C. telescopic gauge
    D. micrometer

16. What is used to attach a thrust plate to an engine block?
    A. Sheet metal screws
    B. Cap screws
    C. Wire spring clips
    D. Stamped metal clips

17. In an *expert* system for offboard computer diagnosis, which stage of knowledge acquisition in developing problem-solving rules occurs LAST?
    A. Implementation
    B. Identification
    C. Formalization
    D. Conceptualization

18. All of the following are possible causes of incorrect steering axis inclination and toe-out figures EXCEPT
    A. worn tires
    B. bent suspension
    C. worn ball joint
    D. worn steering parts

19. In a magnetic circuit, reluctance is a quality that is analogous to the _____ of an electrical circuit.
    A. capacitance
    B. voltage
    C. amperage
    D. resistance

19.____

20. Which device is used MAINLY to check for both open and short circuits?
    A. Short finder
    B. Jumper wires
    C. Test light
    D. Continuity tester

20.____

21. Which type of spring is MOST commonly used in automotive suspension systems?
    A. Torsion bar
    B. Coil spring
    C. Multiple-leaf spring
    D. Monoleaf spring

21.____

22. At the most basic level, the special type of language used to form micro-computer instructions, such as the ones used in automotive controls and diagnostics, is known as
    A. digital coding
    B. assembly language
    C. branch language
    D. fault coding

22.____

23. Most automotive camshafts are made from
    A. hardened alloy cast-iron
    B. steel'
    C. sintered iron
    D. tempered aluminum alloy

23.____

24. What progressively increasing quality should be indicated by a combustion tester as an engine accelerates from idle to cruising speeds?
    A. Higher rate of combustion
    B. Higher fuel-air ratio
    C. Lower thermal efficiency
    D. Leaner fuel mixture

24.____

25. What sizing process conforms metal to size by applying pressure?
    A. Stamping
    C. Burnishing
    C. Canting
    D. Beading

25.____

KEY (CORRECT ANSWERS)

1. D
2. A
3. A
4. C
5. A

6. D
7. C
8. C
9. C
10. A

11. B
12. B
13. B
14. C
15. D

16. B
17. A
18. A
19. D
20. D

21. B
22. B
23. A
24. D
25. B

GLOSSARY OF AUTOMOTIVE TERMS

CONTENTS

	Page
AC ...... Backlash	1
Baffle ...... Circuit	2
Circuit breaker ...... Cylinder block	3
Cylinder head ...... Filter	4
Final drive ...... Hydraulic valve tappet	5
Hydromatic ...... Leverage	6
L-head ...... Overrunning cluth	7
Parabolic reflector ...... Ring gear	8
Rock position ...... Suspension	9
Swaybar ...... Two-stroke-cycle engine	10
Universal joint ..... Worm gear	11

GLOSSARY OF AUTOMOTIVE TERMS

AC—Alternating current, or current that reverses its direction at regular intervals.

Accelerating pump—A device in the carburetor that supplies an additional amount of fuel, temporarily enriching the fuel-air mixture when the throttle is suddenly opened.

Acceleration—The process of increasing velocity. Average rate of change of increasing velocity, usually in feet per second.

Ackerman steering—The steering-system design that permits the front wheels to round a turn without sideslip by turning the inner wheel in more than the outer wheel.

Air bleed—A passage in the carburetor through which air can seep or bleed into fuel moving through a fuel passage.

Air brakes—Vehicle brakes actuated by air pressure.

Air cleaner—A device, mounted on the carburetor or connected to the carburetor, through which air must pass before entering the carburetor air horn. A filtering device in the air cleaner removes dust and dirt particles from the air.

Air-cooled engine—An engine cooled by air circulating between cylinders and around cylinder head as opposed to the liquid-cooled engine cooled by a liquid passing through jackets surrounding the cylinders.

Air filter—A filter through which air passes, and which removes dust and dirt particles from the air. Air filters are placed in passages through which air must pass, as in crankcase breather, air cleaner, etc.

Air horn—That part of the air passage in the carburetor which is on the atmospheric side of the venturi. The choke valve is located in the air horn.

Air-pac brakes—A type of braking system using a vacuum.

Ammeter—An electric meter that measures current, in amperes, in an electric circuit.

Ampere—Unit of electric-current-flow measurement. The current that will flow through a 1-ohm resistance when 1 volt is impressed across the resistance.

Amphibious vehicle—A vehicle with a hull that permits it to float in water, and tracks or wheels that permit it to travel on land.

Angle of approach—The maximum angle of an incline onto which a vehicle can move from a horizontal plane without interference; as, for instance, from front bumpers.

Angle of departure—The maximum angle of an incline from which a vehicle can move onto a horizontal plane without interference; as, for instance, from rear bumpers.

Antifreeze—A substance added to the coolant system in a liquid-cooled-engine to prevent freezing.

Antifriction bearing—A bearing of the type that supports the imposed load on rolling surfaces (balls, rollers, needles), minimizing friction.

Antiknock—Refers to substances that are added to automotive fuel to decrease the tendency to knock when fuel-air mixture is compressed and ignited in the engine cylinder.

Armature—The rotating assembly in a direct current generator or motor. Also, the iron piece in certain electrical apparatus that completes a magnetic (and in many cases, an electric) circuit.

Atmosphere—The mass of air that surrounds the earth.

Atmospheric pressure—The weight of the atmosphere per unit area.

Atom—The smallest particle, or part, of an element, composed of electrons and protons and also of neutrons (with exception of hydrogen).

Atomization—The spraying of a liquid through a nozzle so that the liquid is broken into tiny globules or particles.

Automatic choke—A choke that operates automatically in accordance with certain engine conditions (usually temperature and intake manifold vacuum) (also electrically controlled).

Automatic transmission—A transmission that reduces or eliminates the necessity of handshifting of gears to secure different gear ratios in the transmission.

Axial—In a direction parallel to the axis. Axial movement is movement parallel to the axis.

Axis—A center line. The line about which something rotates or about which something is evenly divided.

Axle—A cross support on a vehicle on which supporting wheel, or wheels, turn. There are two general types: live axles that also transmit power to the wheels and dead axles that transmit no power.

Backfiring—Pre-explosion of fuel-air mixture so that explosion passes back around the opened intake valve and flashes back through the intake manifold.

Backlash—The backward rotation of driven gear that is permitted by clearance between meshing teeth of two gears.

Baffle—A plate or shield to divert the flow of liquid or gas.

Ball bearing—A type of bearing which contains steel balls that roll between inner and outer races.

Battery—A device consisting of two or more cells for converting chemical energy into electrical energy.

Battery charging—The process of supplying a battery with a flow of electric current to produce chemical actions in the battery; these actions reactivate the chemicals in the battery so they can again produce electrical energy.

BDC—Bottom dead center; the position of the piston when it reaches the lower limit of travel in the cylinder.

Bearing—A part in which a journal pivot, or pin turns or revolves. A part on or in which another part slides.

Bendix drive—A type of drive used in a starter which provides automatic coupling with the engine flywheel for cranking and automatic uncoupling when the engine starts.

Bevel gear—One of a pair of meshing gears whose working surfaces are inclined to the center lines of the driving and driven shafts.

Blackout lights—A lamp installed on a vehicle for use during blackouts, which can be seen from the air only at very close range.

Block—See Cylinder block.

Blow-by—Leakage of the compressed fuel-air mixture or burned gases from combustion, passing piston and rings and into the crankcase.

Blower—A mechanical device for compressing and delivering air to engine at higher than atmospheric pressure.

Body—The assembly of sheet-metal sections, framework, doors, windows, etc., which provides an enclosure for passengers or carriage space for freight.

Bogie—A suspension unit consisting of tandem axles jointed by a single cross support (trunnion axle) that also acts as a vertical pivot for the entire unit.

Bond—To bind together.

Bore—The diameter of engine cylinder hole. Also diameter of any hole; as, for example, the hole into which a bushing is fitted.

Boss—An extension or strengthened section, such as the projections within a piston which supports the piston pin.

Brake band—A flexible band, usually of metal with an inner lining of brake fabric, which is tightened on a drum to slow or stop drum rotation.

Brakedrum—Metal drum mounted on car wheel or other rotating members; brake shoes or brake band, mechanically forced against it, causes it to slow or stop.

Brake fluid—A compounded fluid used in hydraulic braking system; it transmits hydraulic force from the brake master cylinder to the wheel cylinder and should be impervious to heat or freezing.

Brake lining—A special woven fabric material with which brake shoes or brake bands are lined: it withstands high temperatures and pressures.

Brakeshoes—The curved metal part, faced with brake lining, which is forced against the brake drum to produce braking or retarding action.

Brake system—The system on a vehicle that slows or stops it as a pedal or lever is operated.

Brake horsepower—The power actually delivered by the engine which is available for driving the vehicle.

Brakes—The mechanism that slows or stops a vehicle or mechanism when a pedal or other control is operated. Also called the *brake system*.

Bronze—An alloy consisting essentially of copper and tin.

Brushes—The carbon or carbon and metal parts in a motor or generator that contact the rotating armature commutator or rings.

Bushing—A sleeve placed in a bore to serve as a bearing surface.

Bypass—A separate passage which permits a liquid, gas, or electric current to take a path other than that normally used.

Cab—Separate driver's compartment provided on trucks.

Cam—A moving part of an irregular form designed to move or alter the motion of another part.

Camber—To curve or bend; the amount in inches or degrees that the front wheels of an automotive vehicle are tilted from a true vertical at the top.

Capacitance—That property of a circuit which tends to increase the amount of current flowing in a circuit for a given voltage or to delete in its entirety.

Capacitor (condenser)—A device for inserting the property of capacitance into a circuit; two or more conductors separated by a dielectric.

Carbon-pile regulator—A type of regulator for regulating or controlling voltage or amperage in a circuit, which makes use of a stack, or pile, of carbon disks.

Carburetor—The device in a fuel system which mixes fuel and air and delivers the combustible mixture to the intake manifold.

Caster—The amount in degrees that the steering knuckle pivots are tilted forward or backward from a true vertical.

Cell—A combination of electrodes and electrolyte which converts chemical energy into electrical energy. Two or more cells connected together form a battery.

Centrifugal advance—The mechanism in an ignition distributor by which the spark is advanced or retarded as the engine speed varies.

Centrifugal force—The force acting on a rotating body, which tends to move its parts outward and away from the center of rotation.

Charge indicator—The device on a vehicle that indicates, by a needle, whether or not the battery is receiving a charge from the generator.

Charging rate—The rate of flow, in amperes, of electric current flowing through a battery while it is being charged.

Chassis—An assembly of mechanisms, attached to a frame, that make up the major operating part of an automotive vehicle (less body).

Choke—A device in the carburetor that chokes off, or reduces, the flow of air into the intake manifold; this produces a partial vacuum in the intake manifold and a consequent richer fuel-air mixture.

Circuit—A closed path or combination of paths through which passage of the medium (electric current, air, liquid, etc.) is possible.

Circuit breaker—In electric circuits, a mechanism designed to break or open the circuit when certain conditions exist; especially the device in automotive circuits that opens the circuit between the generator and battery to prevent overcharging of the battery. (One of the three units comprising a generator regulator.)

Clockwise—Direction of movement, usually rotary, which is the same as movement of hands on the face of a clock.

Clutch—The mechanism in an automotive vehicle, located in the power train, that connects the engine to, or disconnects the engine from, the remainder of the power train.

Coil—In electrical circuits, turns of wire, usually on a core and enclosed in a case, through which electric current passes.

Coil spring—A type of spring made of an elastic metal such as steel, formed into a wire or bar and wound into a coil.

Combat vehicle—A type of vehicle, usually armored, for use in armed combat.

Combustion—A chemical action, or burning; in an engine, the burning of a fuel-air mixture in the combustion chamber.

Combustion chamber—The space at the top of the cylinder and in the head in which combustion of the fuel-air mixture takes place.

Commutation—The process of converting alternating current which flows in the armature windings of direct current generators into direct current.

Commutator—That part of rotating machinery which makes electrical contact with the brushes and connects the armature windings with the external circuit.

Compression—Act of pressing into a smaller space or reducing in size or volume by pressure.

Compression ratio—The ratio between the volume in the cylinder with the piston at bottom dead center and with the piston at top dead center.

Compression rings—The upper rings on a piston; the rings designed to hold the compression in the cylinder and prevent blow-by.

Compression stroke—The piston stroke from bottom dead center to top dead center during which both valves are closed and the gases in the cylinder are compressed.

Concentric—Having a common center, as circles or spheres, one within the other.

Condenser—*See* Capacitor.

Conductor—A material through which electricity will readily flow.

Conecting rod—Linkage between the crankshaft and piston, usually attached to the piston by a piston pin and to the crank journal on the crankshaft by a split bearing and bearing cap.

Coolant—The liquid that circulates in an engine cooling system which reduces heat generated by the engine.

Cooling fan—The fan in the engine cooling system that provides a forced circulation of air through the radiator or around the engine cylinders so that cooling is effected.

Cooling fins—Thin metal projections on air-cooled-engine cylinder and head which greatly increases the heat-radiating surfaces and helps provide cooling of engine cylinder.

Cooling system—A system which reduces heat generated by the engine and thereby prevents engine overheating; includes, in liquid cooled engine, engine water jackets, radiator, and water pump.

Core—An iron mass, generally the central portion of a coil or electromagnet or armature around which the wire is coiled.

Counterclockwise—Direction of movement, usually rotary, which is opposite in direction to movement of hands on the face of a clock.

Cowl—The front portion of the vehicle body or cab which partially incloses the dash panel and forms the windshield frame.

Crank—A device for converting reciprocating motion into rotary motion, and vice versa.

Crankcase—The lower part of the engine in which the crankshaft rotates. In automotive practice, the upper part is lower section of cylinder block while lower section is the oil pan.

Crankcase breather—The opening or tube that allows air to enter the crankcase and thus permit crankcase ventilation.

Crankcase dilution—Dilution of the lubricating oil in the oil pan by liquid gasoline seeping down the cylinder walls past the piston rings.

Crankcase ventilation—The circulation of air through the crankcase which removes water and other vapors, thereby preventing the formation of water sludge and other unwanted substances.

Cranking motor—*See* Starter.

Crankshaft—The main rotating member or shaft of the engine, with cranks to which the connecting rods are attached.

Cross-drive transmission—A special type of transmission used in tanks and other heavy vehicles which combines the actions of a transmission with torque converter, steering system, and differential.

Current regulator—A magnetic-controlled relay by which the field circuit of the generator is made and broken very rapidly to secure even current output from the generator and prevent generator overload from excessive output. (One of the three units comprising a generator regulator.)

Cutout relay—An automatic magnetic switch attached to the generator to cut out generator circuit and prevent overcharging of battery. *See* Circuit breaker.

Cycle—A series of events with a start and finish, during which a definite train of events takes place. In the engine, the four piston strokes (or two piston strokes on 2-stroke cycle engine) that complete the working process and produce power.

Cylinder—A tubular-shaped structure. In the engine, the tubular opening in which the piston moves up and down.

Cylinder block—That part of an engine to which, and in which, other engine parts and accessories are attached or assembled.

Cylinder head—The part of the engine that encloses the cylinder bores. Contains water jackets (on liquid-cooled engine) and valves (on I-head engines).

Dc—Direct current, or current that flows in one direction only.

Damper—A device for reducing the motion or oscillations of moving parts, air, or liquid.

Dash panel—The partition that separates the driver's compartment from the engine compartment. Sometimes called firewall.

Dead axle—An axle that simply supports and does not turn or deliver power to the wheel or rotating member.

Deceleration—The process of slowing down. Opposite to acceleration.

Degasser—A device used in connection with carburetors for shutting off the flow of fuel during deceleration so that gases from incomplete combustion during deceleration are prevented.

Detonation—In the engine, excessively rapid burning of the compressed fuel-air mixture so that knocking results.

Diaphragm—A flexible membrane, usually made of fabric and rubber in automotive components, clamped at the edges and usually spring-loaded; used in fuel pump, vacuum pump, distributor, etc.

Diesel engine—An engine using the diesel cycle of operation; air alone is compressed and diesel fuel is injected at the end of the compression stroke. Heat of compression produces ignition.

Differential—A mechanism between axles that permits one axle to turn at a different speed than the other and, at the same time, transmits power from the driving shaft to the axles.

Differential winding—In electrical machinery, a winding that is wound in a reverse direction or different direction than the main operating windings. The differential winding acts to modify or change the action of the machine under certain conditions.

Disk brake—A type of brake which depends upon contact between two or more disks for its effect. One or more of the disks may be faced with brake lining.

Distributor—See Ignition distributor.

Dolly—A two-wheel trailer coupled to a semitrailer to support and steer its front end when it is converted into a full trailer.

Drag link—An intermediate link in the steering system between the Pitman arm and an intermediate arm, or drag-link arm.

Dual ignition—Ignition system using two spark plugs for each cylinder so that a dual spark effect takes place driving each power stroke.

Dual-ratio axles—Axle in truck which contains a mechanism for changing driving ratio of the wheels to either high or low ratio. Two-speed differential.

Dynamometer—A device for measuring power output of an engine.

Eccentric—Offcenter.

Eddy currents—Currents which are induced in an iron core and circulate in the core.

Efficiency—Ratio between the effect produced and the power expended to produce the effect.

Electric brakes—A brake system which uses electric current for energization.

Electrical system—In the automotive vehicle, the system that electrically cranks the engine for starting, furnishes high-voltage sparks to the engine cylinders to fire compressed fuel-air charges, lights the lights, operates heater motor, radio, etc. Consists, in part, of starter, wiring, battery, generator, generator regulator, ignition distributor, and ignition coil.

Electricity—A form of energy that involves the movement of electrons from one place to another, or the gathering of electrons in one area.

Electrode—Either terminal of an electric source; either conductor by which the current enters and leaves an electrolyte.

Electrolyte—The liquid in a battery or other electrochemical device, in which the conduction of electricity is accompanied by chemical decomposition.

Electromagnet—Temporary magnet constructed by winding a number of turns of insulated wire into a coil or around an iron core; it is energized by a flow of electric current through the coil.

Electron—Negative charged particle that is a basic constituent of matter and electricity. Movement of electrons is an electric current.

Energy—The capacity for performing work.

Engine—An assembly that burns fuel to produce power, sometimes referred to as the power plant.

Evaporation—The action that takes place when a liquid changes to a vapor or gas.

Exhaust manifold—That part of the engine that provides a series of passages through which burned gases from the engine cylinders may flow to the muffler.

Exhaust stroke—The piston stroke from bottom dead center to top dead center during which the exhaust valve is opened so that burned gases are forced from the engine cylinder.

Exhaust valve—The valve which opens to allow the burned gases to escape from the cylinder during the exhaust stroke.

Fan—See Cooling fan.

F-head—A type of engine with valves arranged to form an "F;" one valve is in the head, the other in the cylinder block.

Field—In a generator or electric motor the area in which a magnetic flow occurs.

Field coil—A coil of wire, wound around an iron core, which produces the magnetic field in a generator or motor when current passes through it.

Field frame—The frame in a generator or motor into which the field coils are assembled.

Field winding—See Field coil.

Fifth wheel—The flat, round heavy steel plates (upper and lower) together with a kingpin for coupling semitrailer to truck-tractor. The lower plate is mounted on the truck-tractor, the upper on the semitrailer.

Filter—A devise through which gas or liquid is passed; dirt, dust, and other impurities are removed by the separating action.

Final drive—That part of the power train on tractors, truck-tractors tanks, and tank-like vehicles that carries the driving power to the wheels or sprockets to produce the vehicle motion as they turn.

Float—In the carburetor, the metal shell that is suspended by the fuel in the float bowl and controls a needle valve that regulates the fuel level in the bowl.

Float circuit—In the carburetor, the circuit that controls entry of fuel and fuel level in the float bowl.

Fluid coupling—A coupling in the power train that connects between the engine and other power train members through a fluid.

Flywheel—The rotating metal wheel, attached to the crankshaft, that helps level out the power surges from the power strokes and also serves as part of the clutch and engine-cranking system.

Foot-pound—A unit of work done in raising 1 pound avoirdupois against the force of gravity to the height of 1 foot.

Force—The action that one body may exert upon another to change its motion or shape.

Four-stroke-cycle engine—An engine that requires four piston strokes (intake, compression, power, exhaust) to make the complete cycle of events in the engine cylinder.

Frame—An assembly of metal structural parts and channel sections that support the engine and body and that is supported by the vehicle wheels.

Frequency—The number of vibrations, cycles, or changes in direction in a unit of time.

Friction—The resistance to motion between two bodies in contact with each other.

Fuel—The substance that is burned to produce heat and create motion of the piston on the power stroke in an engine.

Fuel filter—A device placed in the fuel line of the fuel system to remove dirt and other harmful solids.

Fuel gage—An indicating device in the fuel system that indicates the amount of fuel in the fuel tank.

Fuel line—The tube or tubes connecting the fuel tank and the carburetor and through which the fuel passes.

Fuel passage—Drilled holes in the carburetor body and tubes through which fuel passes from the float bowl to the fuel nozzles.

Fuel pump—The mechanism in the fuel system that transfers fuel from the fuel tank to the carburetor.

Fuel tank—The storage tank for fuel on the vehicle.

Fulcrum—The support, as a wedge-shaped piece or a hinge, about which a lever turns.

Full trailer—An independent and fully contained vehicle without motive power.

Fuse—A circuit-protecting device which makes use of a substance that has a low melting point. The substance melts if an overload occurs, thus protecting other devices in the system.

Gasket—A flat strip, usually of cork or metal, or both, placed between two surfaces to provide a tight seal between them.

Gasoline—A hydrocarbon, obtained from petroleum, is suitable as an internal combustion engine fuel.

Gear ratio—The relative speeds at which two gears turn; the proportional rate of rotation.

Gears—Mechanical devices to transmit power or turning effort, from one shaft to another; more specifically, gears which contain teeth that engage or mesh upon turning.

Gearshift—A mechanism by which the gears in a transmission system are engaged.

Generator—In the electrical system, the device that changes mechanical energy to electrical energy for lighting lights, charging the battery, etc.

Generator regulator—In the electrical system, the unit which is composed of the current regulator voltage regulator, and circuit breaker relay.

Governor—A mechanism that controls speed or other variable. Specifically, speed governors used on automotive vehicles to prevent excessive engine speed by controlling actions in the carburetor.

Ground—Connection of an electrical unit to the engine or frame to return the current to its source.

Gusset plate—A plate at the joint of a frame structure of steel to strengthen the joint.

Half track—A vehicle using tracks instead of wheels at the rear.

Handbrake—A brake operated by hand. Also referred to as the parking brake.

Headlight—Lights at the front of the vehicle designed to illuminate the road ahead when the vehicle is traveling forward.

Heat—A form of energy.

Helical—In the shape of a helix, which is the shape of a screw thread or coil spring.

High-speed circuit—In the carburetor, the passages through which fuel flows when the throttle valve is fully opened.

High tension—Another term for high voltage. In the electrical system, refers to the ignition secondary circuit since this circuit produces high-voltage surges to cause sparking at the spark plugs.

Hill holder—A device in the transmission that automatically prevents the vehicle from rolling backwards down a hill when the vehicle is brought to a stop.

Horn—An electrical signaling device on the vehicle.

Horsepower—A measure of a definite amount of power; 550 foot-pound per second.

Hotchkiss drive—Type of rear live axle suspension in which the springs serve as torque members.

Hull—In a tank, the protective shell that encloses the vehicle components and occupants.

Hydraulic brakes—A braking system that uses a fluid to transmit hydraulic pressure from a master cylinder to wheel cylinders, which then cause brakeshoe movement and braking action.

Hydraulic steering—A steering sysem that uses a fluid to produce an assisting hydraulic pressure on the steering linkage, thus reducing the steering effort on the part of the driver.

Hydraulic traversing mechanism—A turret traversing system that makes use of hydraulic pressure to furnish the motive power to traverse the turret.

Hydraulic valve tappet—A valve tappet that, by means of hydraulic pressure, maintains zero valve clearance so that valve noise is reduced.

Hydramatic—A type of automatic transmission containing a fluid coupling and automatic controls for shifting from one gear ratio to another.

Hydrometer—A device to determine the specific gravity of a liquid. This indicates the freezing point of the coolant in a cooling system or, as another example, the state of charge of a battery.

Hydrovac brakes—A type of braking system using vacuum to assist in brake operation. The vacuum action reduces the effort required from the driver to operate the vehicle brakes.

Idle—Engine speed when accelerator pedal is fully released; generally assumed to mean when engine is doing no work.

Idle circuit—The circuit in the carburetor through which fuel is fed when the engine is idling.

Idler gear—A gear placed between a driving and a driven gear to make them rotate in the same direction. It does not affect the gear ratio.

Idling adjustment—Adjustment made on the carburetor to alter the fuel-air mixture ratio or engine speed on idle.

Ignition—The action of setting fire to; in the engine, the initiating of the combustion process in the engine cylinders.

Ignition advance—Refers to the spark advance produced by the distributor in accordance with engine speed and intake manifold vacuum.

Ignition coil—That component of the ignition system that acts as a transformer and steps up battery voltage to many thousand volts; the high voltage then produces a spark at the spark-plug gap.

Ignition distributor—That component of the ignition system that closes and opens the circuit between the battery and ignition coil, and distributes the resultant high-voltage surges from the coil to the proper spark plugs.

Ignition switch—The switch in the ignition system that can be operated to open or close the ignition primary circuit.

Ignition timing—Refers to the timing of the spark at the spark plug as related to the piston position in the engine cylinder.

I-head—A type of engine with valves in the cylinder head.

Impeller—The rotor of a centrifugal pump which causes the fuel-air in an engine to be thrown into a diffuser chamber to effect thorough mixing and good distribution.

Indicated horsepower—A measurement of engine power based on power actually developed in the engine cylinders.

Induction—The action or process of producing voltage by the relative motion of a magnetic field and a conductor.

Injector—The mechanism, including nozzle, which injects fuel into the engine combustion chamber on diesel engines.

In-line engine—An engine in which all engine cylinders are in a single row, or line.

Insert—A form of screw thread insert to be placed in a tapped hole into which a screw or bolt will be screwed. The insert protects the part into which the hole was tapped, preventing enlargement due to repeated removal and replacement of the bolt.

Insulation—Substance that stops movement of electricity (electrical insulation) or heat (heat insulation).

Insulator—A substance (usually of glass or porcelain) that will not conduct electricity.

Intake manifold—That component of the engine which provides a series of passages from the carburetor to the engine cylinders through which fuel-air mixture can flow.

Intake stroke—The piston stroke from top dead center to bottom dead center during which the intake valve is open and the cylinder receives a charge of fuel-air mixture.

Intake valve—The valve in the engine which is opened during the intake stroke to permit the entrance of fuel-air mixture into the cylinder.

Integral—Whole; entire; lacking nothing of completeness.

Interference—In radio, any signal received that overrides or prevents normal reception of the desired signal. In mechanical practice, anything that causes mismating of parts so they cannot be normally assembled.

Internal combustion engine—An engine in which the fuel is burned inside the engine, as opposed to an external combustion engine where the fuel is burned outside the engine, such as a steam engine.

Internal gear—A gear in which the teeth point inward rather than outward as with a standard spur gear.

Jackshaft—An intermediate driving shaft.

Jet—A metered opening in an air or fuel passage to control the flow of fuel or air.

Journal—That part of a shaft that rotates in a bearing.

Kingpin—The pin by which a stud axle is articulated to an axle-beam or steering head; also the enmeshing pin in a fifth wheel assembly.

Kingpin inclination—The number of degrees that the kingpin, which supports the front wheel, is tilted from the vertical.

Knock—In the engine, a rapping or hammering noise resulting from excessively rapid burning or detonation of the compressed fuel-air mixture.

Knuckle—A joint or parts carrying a hinge pin which permit one part to swing about or move in relation to another.

Laminated—Made up of thin sheets, leaves, or plates.

Laminated leaf spring—Spring made up of leaves of graduated size.

Landing gear—Retractable support under the front end of a semitrailer to hold it up when it is uncoupled from the truck tractor.

Lean mixture—A fuel-air mixture that has a high proportion of air and a low proportion of fuel.

Lever—A rigid bar or beam of any shape capable of turning about one point, called the fulcrum; used for transmitting or changing force or motion.

Leverage—The mechanical advantage obtained by use of lever; also an arrangement or combination of levers.

L-head—A type of engine with valves in the cylinder block.

Light—In the electric circuit, an electrical device that includes a wire in a gas-filled bulb which glows brightly when current passes through it—often called a lamp.

Lighting switch—In the electrical circuit, a switch that turns light on or off.

Lubrication—The process of supplying a coating of oil between moving surfaces to prevent actual contact between them. The oil film permits relative movement with little frictional resistance.

Lunette—An eye that hooks into a pintle assembly to tow vehicles.

Magnet—Any body that has the ability to attract iron.

Magnetic field—The space around a magnet which the magnetic lines of force permeate.

Magnetic flux—The total amount of magnetic induction across or through a given surface.

Magnetic pole—Focus of magnetic lines of force entering or emanating from magnet.

Magnetism—The property exhibited by certain substances and produced by electron (or electric current) motion which results in the attraction of iron.

Magneto—A device that generates voltage surges, transforms them to high-voltage surges, and distributes them to the engine cylinder spark plugs.

Main bearing—In the engine, the bearings that support the crankshaft.

Manifold—*See* Intake manifold or exhaust manifold.

Master cylinder—In the hydraulic braking system, the liquid-filled cylinder in which hydraulic pressure is developed by depression of the brake pedal.

Master rod—In a radial engine, the rod to which all other connecting rods are attached, or articulated.

Matter—Anything which has weight and occupies space.

Mechanical efficiency—In an engine, the ratio between brake horsepower and indicated horsepower.

Mechanism—A system of parts or appliances which acts as a working agency to achieve a desired result.

Member—Any essential part of a machine or structure.

Meshing—The mating or engaging of the teeth of two gears.

Metering rod—A small rod, having a varied diameter, operated within a jet to vary the flow of fuel through the jet.

Molecule—The smallest particle into which a chemical compound can be divided.

Motor—A device for converting electrical energy into mechanical energy.

Motorcycle—Two-wheeled vehicle similar to a bicycle but motor-driven.

Motor tricycle—Similar to a motorcycle except the rear wheel has been replaced by two wheels.

Muffler—In the exhaust system, a device through which the exhaust gases must pass; in the muffler, the exhaust sounds are greatly reduced.

Mutual induction—Induction associated with more than one circuit, as two coils, one of which induces current in the other as the current in the first changes.

Negative—A term designating the point of lower potential when the potential difference between two points is considered.

Negative terminal—The terminal from which electrons depart when a circuit is completed from this terminal to the positive terminal of generator or battery.

Needle valve—Type of valve with rod-shaped, needle-pointed valve body which works into a valve seat so shaped that the needle point fits into it and closes the passage; the needle valve in the carburetor float circuit is an example.

North pole—The pole of a magnet from which the lines of force are assumed to emanate.

No-spin differential—A special type of differential which prevents the spinning of one of the driving wheels even if it is resting on smooth ice.

Nozzle—An orifice or opening in a carburetor through which fuel feeds into the passing air stream on its way to the intake manifold.

Octane rating—A measure of the antiknock value of engine fuel.

Odometer—The part of the speedomter that measures, accumulatively, the number of vehicle miles traveled.

Ohm—A measure of electrical resistance. A conductor of one ohm resistance will allow a flow of one ampere of current when one volt is imposed on it.

Ohmmeter—A device for measuring ohms resistance of a circuit or electrical machine.

Oil—A liquid lubricant derived from petroleum and used in machinery to provide lubrication between moving parts. Also, fuel used in diesel engines.

Oil control rings—The lower rings on the piston which are designed to prevent excessive amounts of oil from working up into the combustion chamber.

Oil cooler—A special cooling radiator, through which hot oil passes. Air also passes through separate passages in the radiator, providing cooling of the oil.

Oil gage—Indicating device that indicates the pressure of the oil in the lubrication system. Also a bayonet-type rod to measure oil in the crankcase.

Oil pan—The lower part of the crankcase in which a reservoir of oil is maintained.

Oil pump—The pump that transfers oil from the oil pan to the various moving parts in the engine that require lubrication.

Oil strainer—A strainer placed at the inlet end of the oil pump to strain out dirt and other particles, preventing these from getting into moving engine parts.

Overflow tank—Special tank in cooling system (a surge tank) for hot or dry country to permit expansion and contraction of engine coolant without loss.

Overhead valve—Valve mounted in head above combustion chamber. Valve in I-head engine.

Overload breaker—In an electrical circuit, a device that breaks or opens a circuit if it is overloaded by a short, ground, use of too much equipment, etc.

Overrunning clutch—A type of drive mechanism used in a starter which transmits cranking effort but overruns freely when engine tries to drive starter. Also, a special clutch used in several mechanism that permits a rotating member to turn freely under some conditions but not under other conditions.

Parabolic reflector—A reflector that sends all reflected light originating at the focal point outward in parallel rays.

Parallel circuit—The electrical circuit formed when two or more electrical devices have like terminals connected together (positive to positive and negative to negative) so that each may operate independently of the other.

Parking brake—*See* Handbrake.

Period—The time required for the completion of one cycle.

Permanent magnet—Piece of steel or alloy in which molecules are so alined that the piece continues to exhibit magnetism without application of external influence.

Phase—That portion of a whole period which has elapsed since the activity in question passed through zero position in a positive direction.

Pilot—A short plug at the end of a shaft to aline it with another shaft or rotating part.

Pinion—The smaller of two mating or meshing gears.

Pintle assembly—A swivel-type assembly used to engage with a lunette for towing trailers.

Piston—In an engine, the cylindrical part that moves up and down in the cylinder.

Piston displacement—The volume displaced by the piston as it moves from the bottom to the top of the cylinder in one complete stroke.

Piston pin—The cylindrical or tubular metal pin that attaches the piston to the connecting rod (also called wrist pin).

Piston ring—One of the rings fitted into grooves in the piston. There are two types, compression rings and oil-control rings.

Piston rod—*See* Connecting rod.

Pitman arm—The arm that is a part of the steering gear; it is connected by linkage to the wheel steering knuckle.

Pivot inclination—*See* Kingpin inclination.

Planetary gears—Set of gears that includes a central spur gear, called the sun gear, around which revolves one or more meshing planetary gears. An internal gear, meshed with the planetary gears, completes the set.

Poppet—A spring-loaded ball engaging a notch. A ball latch.

Positive—A term designating the point of higher potential when the potential difference between two points is considered.

Potential—A characteristic of a point in an electric field or circuit indicated by the work necessary to bring a unit positive charge from infinity; the degree of electrification as compared to some standard (the earth, for example).

Potential difference—The arithmetical difference between two electrical potentials; same as electromotive force, electrical pressure, or voltage.

Power—The rate of doing work.

Power divider—A mechanism placed between dual rear axles to apportion driving effort between the two pairs of wheels to provide the maximum tractive effort.

Power plant—The engine or power-producing mechanism on the vehicle.

Power steering—Vehicle steering by use of hydraulic pressure to multiply the driver's steering effort so as to improve ease of steering.

Power stroke—The piston stroke from top dead center to bottom dead center during which the fuel-air mixture burns and forces the piston down so the engine produces power.

Power-take-off—An attachment for connecting the engine to power driven auxiliary machinery when its use is required.

Preignition—Premature ignition of the fuel-air mixture being compressed in the cylinder on the compression stroke.

Primer—An auxiliary fuel pump operated by hand to feed additional fuel into the engine to produce a richer mixture for starting.

Prismatic lens—A lens with parallel grooves or flutes which deflect and distribute light rays.

Propeller shaft—The driving shaft in the power train that carries engine power from the transmission to the differential; also, the shaft that turns the propeller in amphibian vehicles.

Proton—Basic particle of matter having a positive electrical charge, normally associated with the nucleus of the atom.

Psi—Pounds per square inch, a measure of force per unit area.

Pump—A device that transfers gas or liquid from one place to another.

Rpm—Revolutions per minute, a measure of rotational speed.

Radial—Pertaining to the radius of a circle.

Radial engine—An engine with each cylinder located on the radius of a circle and with all cylinders disposed around a common crankshaft.

Radiator—A device in the cooling system that removes heat from the coolant passing through it, permitting coolant to remove heat from the engine.

Radius—Distance from the center of a circle or from center of rotation.

Rectifier—An electrical device that changes alternating current to direct current.

Relay—In the electrical system, a device that opens or closes a second circuit in response to voltage or amperage changes in a controlling circuit.

Residual magnetism—The magnetism retained by a material after all magnetizing forces have been removed.

Resistance—The opposition offered by a substance or body to the passage through it of an electric current.

Resistor—In an electrical system, a device made of resistance wire, carbon, or other resisting material, which has a definite value of resistance and serves a definite purpose in the system by virtue of that resistance.

Rheostat—A resistor for regulating the current by means of variable resistance.

Rich mixture—Fuel-air mixture with a high proportion of fuel.

Rim—That part of a vehicle wheel on which the tire is mounted.

Ring gear—A gear in the form of a ring such as the ring gear on a flywheel or differential.

Rock position—The piston and connecting rod position (top or bottom dead center) at which the crank can rock or rotate a few degrees without appreciable movement of the piston.

Rod—*See* Connecting rod.

Rod cap—The lower detachable part of the connecting rod which can be taken off by removing bolts or nuts so the rod can be detached from the crankshaft.

Roller bearing—A type of bearing with rollers positioned between two races.

Rotor—A part that revolves in a stationary part; especially the rotating member of an electrical mechanism.

SAE—Society of Automotive Engineers.

SAE horsepower—A measurement based upon number of cylinders and cylinder diameter.

Scooter—A small version of a motorcycle.

Sealed-beam—A special type of headlight in which the reflector and lens are sealed together to enclose and protect the filaments.

Self-induction—A property of a circuit which causes it to magnetically affect voltage and current in the circuit.

Semitrailer—A type of trailer supported at the rear by attached wheels and at the front by the truck-tractor; the truck-tractor can be coupled and uncoupled by means of fifth wheel.

Separator—In the storage battery, the wood, rubber, or glass mat strip used as insulator to hold the battery plates apart.

Series circuit—The electrical circuit formed when two or more electrical devices have unlike terminals connected together (positive to negative) so that the same current must flow through all.

Shackle—A swinging support that permits a leaf spring to vary in length as it is deflected.

Shim—A strip of copper or similar material, used under a bearing cap for example, to adjust bearing clearance.

Shimmy—Abnormal sidewise vibration, particularly of the front wheels.

Shock absorber—A device placed at a vehicle wheel to regulate spring rebound and compression.

Short circuit—In electrical circuits, an abnormal connection that permits current to take a short path or circuit, thus by-passing important parts of the normal circuit.

Shroud—Forward subassembly of a body or cab containing dash, cowl, and instrument panel. Also, a hood placed around a fan to improve fan action.

Shunt—Parallel connections, in a portion of an electrical circuit.

Side car—A car attached to a motorcycle for carrying a passenger or cargo.

Slip joint—In the power train, a variable-length connection that permits the propeller shaft to change effective length.

Solenoid—A coil of wire that exhibits magnetic properties when electric current passes through it.

South pole—The pole of the magnet into which it is assumed the magnetic lines of force pass.

Spark plug—The assembly that includes a pair of electrodes which has the purpose of providing a spark gap in the engine cylinder.

Specific gravity—The ratio of the weight of a substance to weight of an equal volume of chemically pure water at 39.2° F.

Speed—Rate of motion.

Speedometer—An indicating device, usually connected to the transmission, that indicates the speed of motion of the vehicle.

Spider—In planetary gear sets, the frame, or part, on which the planetary gears are mounted.

Spiral bevel gear—A bevel gear having curved teeth.

Spline—Slot or groove cut in a shaft or bore; a splined shaft onto which a hub, wheel, etc., with matching splines in its bore is assembled so the two must engage and turn together.

Sprag unit—A form of overrunning clutch; power can be transmitted through it in one direction but not in the other.

Springs—Flexible or elastic members that support the weight of a vehicle.

Spur gear—A gear with radial teeth parallel to the axis.

Starter—In the electrical system, the motor that cranks the engine to get it started.

Starting system—The electrical system, including the starter battery, cables, switch and controls, that has the job of starting the engine.

Static electricity—Accumulated electrical charges, usually considered to be those produced by friction.

Steering gear—That part of the steering system, located at the lower end of the steering shaft, which carries the rotary motion of the steering wheel to the vehicle wheels for steering.

Steering geometry—Difference in angles between the two front wheels and the car frame during turns; the inside wheel turns more sharply than the other wheel turns since it must travel on an arc of a smaller radius. Also called *toe-out during turns*.

Steering linkage—Linkage between steering gear and vehicle wheels.

Steering system—The system of gears and linkage in the vehicle that permits the driver to turn the wheels for changing the direction of vehicle movement.

Storage battery—A lead-acid electrochemical device that changes chemical energy into electric energy. The action is reversible; electric energy supplied to the battery stores chemical energy.

Stroke—The movement, or the distance of the movement, in either direction, of the piston travel in an engine.

Sulfation—A crystalline formation of lead sulfate on storage battery plates.

Sun gear—In a planetary gear system, the central gear.

Supercharger—A device used in connection with engine fuel-air systems to supply more air at greater pressure to the engine, thereby increasing volumetric efficiency.

Suppression—In the electrical system, the elimination of stray electromagnetic waves due to action of ignition, generator, etc., so that they cannot be detected by radio.

Suspension—The system of springs, etc., supporting the upper part of a vehicle on its axles or wheels.

Swaybar—A connecting bar placed between wheel supports, parallel to the axles, which prevents excessive vehicle roll or sway on turns.

Switch—In the electrical system, a device used to open or complete an electrical circuit.

Synchromesh—A name designating a certain type of transmission which has the virtue of permitting gear-ratio shifts without gear clashing.

Synchronize—To make two or more events or operations occur at the same time.

Tachometer—A device for measuring revolutions per minute.

Tactical vehicle—Vehicle designated primarily to meet field requirements in direct connection with combat, tactical operations, and the training of troops for combat.

Tandem axles—Two axles one placed directly in front of the other.

Taper—To make gradually smaller toward one end; a gradual reduction in size in a given direction.

TDC—Top dead center; the position of the piston when it reaches the upper limit of travel in the cylinder.

Temperature gage—An indicating device in the cooling system that indicates the temperature of the coolant and gives warning if excessive engine temperatures develop.

Tension—A stress caused by a pulling force.

Thermal efficiency—Ratio between the power output and the energy in the fuel burned to produce the output.

Thermostat—A device for automatic regulation of temperature.

Third-brush generator—An auxiliary brush which regulates the current output of the generator by increasing or decreasing the field coil current.

Three-quarter trailer—Trailers, usually 2-wheeled; used for light loads. The load is practically balanced on the trailer suspension, although some of the load is thrust on the truck-tractor connection.

Throttle—A mechanism in the fuel system that permits the driver to vary the amount of fuel-air mixture entering the engine and thus control the engine speed.

Throttle valve plate—The disk in the lower part of the carburetor air horn that can be tilted to pass more or less fuel-air mixture to the engine.

Thrust—A force tending to push a body out of alinement. A force exerted endwise through a member upon another member.

Tie rod—A rod connection in the steering system between wheels.

Timing—Refers to ignition or valve timing and pertains to the relation between the actions of the ignition or valve mechanism and piston position in the cylinder.

Tire—The rubber and fabric part that is assembled on the wheel rim and filled with compressed air (pneumatic type).

Toe-in—The amount in inches that the front of the front wheels point inward.

Torqmatic transmission—A special type of transmission which includes a torque converter; it is designed for heavy-vehicle application.

Torque—A twisting or turning effort. Torque is the product of force times the distance, from the center of rotation at which it is exerted.

Torque converter—A special form of fluid coupling in which torque may be increased (at expense of speed).

Torque rod—Arm or rod used to insure accurate alinement of an axle with the frame and to relieve springs of driving and braking stresses.

Torque-tube drive—The type of rear-end arrangement which includes a hollow tube that encloses the propeller shaft and also takes up stresses produced by braking and driving.

Torque wrench—A special wrench with a dial that indicates the amount of torque in pound-feet being applied to a bolt or nut.

Torsional vibration—Vibration in a rotary direction; a portion of a rotating shaft that repeatedly moves ahead, or lags behind, the remainder of the shaft is exhibiting torsional vibration.

Torus—Rotating member of fluid coupling.

Track—The endless tread on which a tank rides.

Tracklaying vehicle—A vehicle that uses tracks instead of wheels for mobility.

Traction—The force exerted in drawing a body along a plane as when a truck-tractor pulls a semitrailer.

Tractive effort—The pushing effort the driving wheels can make against the ground, which is the same as the forward thrust or push of the axles against the vehicle.

Tractor—A motor vehicle (wheeled or tracked) especially designed to tow trailers.

Trailer—A vehicle without motive power towed by a motor vehicle, designed primarily for cargo carrying.

Transfer—The auxiliary assembly for applying power to both forward and rear propeller shafts, and to front wheels as well as rear wheels.

Transmission—The device in the power train that provides different gear ratios between the engine and driving wheels, as well as reverse.

Transmission brake—A brake placed at the rear of the transmission, usually used for parking.

Tread—The design on the road-contacting surface of a tire which provides improved frictional contact.

Truck-tractor—A motor vehicle especially designed to tow semitrailers.

Trunnion—Either of two opposite pivots or cylindrical projections from the sides of a part assembly, supported by bearings, to provide a means of swiveling or turning the part or assembly.

Trunnion axle—A supporting axle which carries a load with other axles attached to it. Its use as a part of a bogie permits independent wheel action in a vertical plane and within designed limits.

Turbine—A mechanism containing a rotor with curved blades; the rotor is driven by the impact of a liquid or gas against the curved blades.

Turret traversing mechanism—A mechanism for rotating a tank turret on a horizontal plane.

Two-stroke-cycle engine—An internal combustion engine requiring but two piston strokes to complete the cycle of events that produce power.

Universal joint—A device that transmits power through an angle.

Unsprung weight—Weight of a vehicle that is not supported by springs.

Vacuum—A space entirely devoid of matter.

Vacuum advance—The mechanism on an ignition distributor that advances the spark in accordance with vacuum in the intake manifold.

Vacuum brakes—Vehicle brakes that are actuated by vacuum under the control of the driver.

Vacuum pump—A pump, used in a vacuum brake system (for example), that produces a vacuum in a designated chamber.

Vacuum switch—In the starting system, an electric switch that is actuated by vacuum to open the starting system control circuit as the engine starts, producing a vacuum in the intake manifold.

Valve—A mechanism that can be opened or closed to allow or stop the flow of a liquid, gas, or vapor from one to another place.

Valve seat—The surface, normally curved, against which the valve operating face comes to rest, to provide a seal against leakage of liquid, gas, or vapor.

Valve seat insert—Metal ring inserted into valve seat; made of special metal that can withstand operating temperature satisfactorily.

Valve spring—The compression-type spring that closes the valve when the valve-operating cam assumes a closed-valve position.

Valve tappet—The part that rides on the valve-operating cam and transmits motion from the cam to the valve stem or push rod.

Valve timing—Refers to the timing of valve closing and opening in relation to piston position in the cylinder.

Valve train—The train of moving parts to the valve that causes valve movement.

Vapor lock—A condition in the fuel system in which gasoline has vaporized, as in the fuel line, so that fuel delivery to the carburetor is blocked or retarded.

Velocity—The rate of motion or speed at any instant, usually measured in miles-per-hour or feet-per-second or minute.

Venturi—In the carburetor, the restriction in the air horn that produces the vacuum responsible for the movement of fuel into the passing air stream.

Vibration—An unceasing back and forth movement over the same path; often with reference to the rapid succession of motions of parts of an elastic body.

Volatility—A measurement of the ease with which a liquid turns to vapor.

Volt—Unit of potential, potential difference, or electrical pressure.

Voltage regulator—A device used in connection with generator to keep the voltage constant and to prevent it from exceeding a predetermined maximum. (One of the three units comprising a generator regulator.)

Volumetric efficiency—Ratio between the amount of fuel-air mixture that actually enters an engine cylinder and the amount that could enter under ideal conditions.

Volute springs—Helical coil springs made from flat steel tapered both in width and thickness.

V-type engine—Engine with two banks of cylinders set at an angle to each other in the shape of a "V."

Wander—To ramble or move without control from a fixed course, as the front wheels of a vehicle.

Water jacket—A jacket that surrounds cylinders and cylinder head, through which coolant flows.

Water manifold—A manifold used to distribute coolant to several points in the cylinder block or cylinder head.

Water pump—In the cooling system, the pump that circulates coolant between the engine water jackets and the radiator.

Wheel alinement—The mechanics of keeping all the parts of the steering system in correct relation with each other.

Wheel brake—A brake that operates at the wheel, usually on a brake drum attached to the wheel.

Wheel cylinder—In hydraulic braking systems, the hydraulic cylinder that operates the brake shoes when hydraulic pressure is applied in the cylinder.

Winch—A mechanism actuating a drum upon which a cable is coiled, so that when a rotating power is applied to the drum, a powerful pull is produced.

Wobble plate—That part of a special type of pump (wobble pump) which drives plungers back and forth as it rotates to produce pumping action. It is a disk, or plate, set at an angle on a rotating shaft.

Work—The result of a force acting against opposition to produce motion. It is measured in terms of the product of the force and the distance it acts.

Worm gear—A gear having concave, helical teeth that mesh with the threads of a worm. Also called a *worm wheel*.

ANSWER SHEET

TEST NO. _____ PART _____ TITLE OF POSITION _____
(AS GIVEN IN EXAMINATION ANNOUNCEMENT - INCLUDE OPTION, IF ANY)

PLACE OF EXAMINATION _____ DATE _____
(CITY OR TOWN) (STATE)

RATING

USE THE SPECIAL PENCIL. MAKE GLOSSY BLACK MARKS.

Make only ONE mark for each answer. Additional and stray marks may be counted as mistakes. In making corrections, erase errors COMPLETELY.